North Wales
in the
Civil War

North Wales
in the
Civil War

Norman Tucker
F.R. Hist. S.

bRidge
books
Wrexham, Clwyd, U.K.

This edition published in Wales by
BRIDGE BOOKS
61 Park Avenue
Wrexham, Clwyd
LL12 7AW

1992

ISBN 1-872424-24-4

Printed and bound by WBC Print Ltd
Bridgend, Mid Glamorgan

ABBREVIATIONS

Phillips.—The Civil War in Wales & the Marches. J. Roland Phillips. (1874).

A. & M.—Ancient and Modern Denbigh. J. Williams. (1856).

Hyde Hall.—A Description of Caernarvonshire (1809-1811).—E. Hyde Hall. Caernarvonshire Historical Society. Record Series. No. 2.

Hall.—A History of Nantwich. J. Hall. (1883).

Chester. Vol. XXV.—The Siege of Chester by the late Canon Rupert Morris, D.D., F.S.A. edited by P. H. Lawson, A.R.I.B.A. — Chester and North Wales Archaeological and History Society Journal, No. XXV. (1923).

Taylor.—Historic Notices of the Borough and County Town of Flint. H. Taylor. (1883).

Newcome.—An account of the Castle and Town of Ruthin. R. Newcome. (1829). An account of the Castle and Town of Denbigh.

Hemingway.—A History of the City of Chester. J. Hemingway. (1831).

C.W.P.—Calendar of Wynn (of Gwydir) Papers. National Library of Wales. (1926).

D.N.B.—Dictionary of National Biography.

Mahler.—The History of Chirk Castle and Chirkland. Margaret Mahler. (1912).

O.P.—The Ottley Papers. Shropshire Archaeological Society.

Cal. S.P.D.—Calendar of State Papers Domestic.

Parry.—Royal Visits and Progresses to Wales. E. Parry (1850).

Arch. Camb.—Archaeologia Cambrensis.

Caerns. H.S. Tr.—Caernarvonshire Historical Society *Transactions.*

Denb. H.S. Tr.—Denbighshire Historical Society *Transactions.*

Flints. H.S. Pub.—Flintshire Historical Society *Publications.*

Palmer (Wrexham Church).—A History of the Parish Church of Wrexham. A. N. Palmer.

Palmer (13) Townships.—The History of the 13 townships of the old parish of Wrexham. A. N. Palmer.

U.C.N.W.—University College of North Wales.

N.L.W.—National Library of Wales.

Aberconwy.—A History of the Antiquities of the Town of Aberconwy. Rev. Robert Williams (1835).

FOREWORD

A TASK of this nature inevitably places a writer under obligation to others. Some authorities have passed on, leaving their labours to speak on their behalf. I have reaped the benefit of the research done by J. Roland Phillips, John Williams of Denbigh, and Archdeacon Richard Newcome whose books are now difficult to obtain. *The Siege of Chester* by the late Canon Rupert Morris contains helpful references to North Wales affairs.

Among living authors the greatest authorities on this period in Wales are Professor A. H. Dodd and Sir Frederick Rees. I should be lacking in gratitude as well as in courtesy if I did not acknowledge my indebtedness to Professor Dodd, not merely for his authoritative works on which I have drawn freely, but for his unfailing kindness whenever I have had occasion to consult him.

The Librarian of the University College of North Wales, Mr. Emyr Gwynne Jones, has graciously allowed me access to manuscripts and reference books. Professor Glyn Roberts has been equally courteous in giving me the benefit of his wisdom. The Caernarvonshire County Archivist, Mr. W. Ogwen Williams, has cheerfully assisted me when I have had occasion to examine ancient records. I have been helped, too, by Mr. E. D. Jones, keeper of manuscripts at the National Library of Wales, and Mr. M. Bevan Evans, County Archivist for Flintshire. The laborious task of fair-copying my typescript has been willingly performed by my wife.

In undertaking this book I have been urged not merely by a desire to draw attention to North Wales's participation in the Civil War, but also by a wish to pay tribute, belated and inadequate though it is, to many brave men whose sacrifices and sufferings have been well nigh forgotten.

Norman Tucker.

1958.

7

CHAPTER ONE

THOUGH the part North Wales played in the Great Rebellion was not conspicuous it was of considerable consequence. With a typically apt phrase that Civil War gossip, Arthur Trevor (half-brother to Sir Marcus Trevor of Brynkinallt) described Wales as 'the nursery of the king's infantry'. The Parliamentary commander-in-chief in Cheshire, Sir William Brereton, regarded Wales as the magazine whence 'all his Majesty's provisions of victualls and men doe proceed'.[1]

If the king lacked sturdy pikemen or musketeers for his hard-pressed foot it was to North Wales the royal eyes instinctively turned. Should Rupert desire footmen for his famous Bluecoats he came to North Wales to recruit. This discomfited prince slept in Ruthin Castle on August 22, 1644, after riding this way to replenish his ranks depleted at Marston Moor. It was the men of North Wales who stormed the barricades at Brentford and helped Rupert to capture Birmingham. It is significant that King Charles, after raising his standard at Nottingham, marched to Shrewsbury, well knowing that he could count on the loyalists in North Wales to swell his ranks. The two visits the king paid to Wrexham early in the campaign indicate the importance he attached to the area.

Whether a survey of the defensive works of North Wales was made at the outset is not known but it is improbable. Provided no landing was attempted by Irish rebels —and there were several alarums—no one anticipated that the tranquil countryside would be disturbed by strife. The issue—so it seemed—would be settled in far-off England. The rebels (every Cavalier was convinced) would never withstand the fiery charges of Rupert's slashing horsemen. People were of one mind—that 'one battle would settle it'.

The Parliament depended on the Militia Acts to supply their army with fighting men; the king operated through the Commission of Array. Which system was more efficacious

---

[1] *Chester.* Vol. XXV. p. 42.

depended on the sentiment which prevailed in an area or on the influence of the leading families.

Flintshire and Denbighshire—at least, east Denbighshire—being nearer the English border were the counties most actively interested in the trend of national events. Though Parliamentary sentiment was not unknown in south Caernarvonshire and round about Wrexham it was not assertive, and North Wales as a whole was regarded as Royalist territory. The loyal baronet of Lleweni represented the shire of Denbigh in the Short Parliament, but Sir Thomas Salusbury stood down at the next election rather than compete with his opulent uncle, Sir Thomas Myddelton of Chirk Castle, who used his wealth and his influence on behalf of the Parliament as soon as he was elected. Simon Thelwall of Plas-y-Ward who represented the borough followed suit and later obtained a commission as colonel of horse.

The area possessed a few professional soldiers such as Colonel Robert Ellice of Gwasnewydd who served under Gustavus Adolphus, Lieut.-Colonel Thomas Davies of Gwysaney who fought in the campaigns of the Thirty Years War, and possibly Sir John Owen of Clenennau, but the majority of the officers were amateur warriors.

The Bishops' Wars provided a mild experiment in calling out local levies. Statistics of the musters are illuminating as they show how recruiting accelerated when the Civil War broke out.

In 1640, Denbigh county raised 200 footmen, Caernarvonshire contributing 160 and Flintshire 80.[2] It was required that there should be 'one drum and drummer for every 100 men.' Each man received 8d. per day during the exercising of the troops. The order that 'a good choice is to be made from the trained bands of men ablebodied and of meet years' indicates that the totals quoted did not exhaust the resources of each county. All men between sixteen and sixty were liable for military service in an emergency. Arms and armour would be stored in a magazine, usually in the

---

[2]C.W.P. 1664.

county town where there was a castle. The strongholds which were to feature in the Civil War were:

FLINTSHIRE: Hawarden, Flint, Rhuddlan.
DENBIGHSHIRE: Holt, Chirk, Ruthin, Denbigh.
CAERNARVONSHIRE: Conway, Caernarvon.
MERIONETH: Harlech.
ANGLESEY: Beaumaris.

Farther off lay Aberystwyth Castle, Montgomery Castle, and Powys Castle—termed Red Castle. Near Beaumaris at Aberlleiniog was a small fortalice known as 'Lady Cheadle's Fort'. Powys Castle was the seat of Lord Powys, and Chirk was the palatial home of Sir Thomas Myddelton. The remaining castles were in a ruinous state, roofs leaking, wood rotting, ramparts crumbling, yet with substantial walls which presented a formidable obstacle.

By this time North Wales had a definite road system though hard surfaces were not known until the coming of the turnpikes a century later. Ogilby in his road map of 1675 shows the main route from Chester passing through Denbigh, Henllan, Llannefydd, Betws-yn-Rhos, and Dolwen to what is now termed 'Glan Conway Corner,' and so to the ferry. He adds: 'Another Road is from Chester to Flint and Holywell then over Rhylan Marsh through Abergely to Conway.' This was the route traversed by Lord Byron's emaciated warriors after the fall of Chester; they were allowed five days to cover the distance to Conway.[3] Ogilby's map marks a gallows on Denbigh Green, Speed depicts one outside Flint; at Beaumaris the name of Gallows Point is a reminder of a county town's function in the olden days. A few fishing-boats and barks engaged in coastal trade were to be found at Conway, Beaumaris and Caernarvon.

The market towns were:

FLINTSHIRE: Flint, Rhuddlan.
DENBIGHSHIRE: Denbigh, Ruthin, Llangollen, Wrexham.
CAERNARVONSHIRE: Conway, Bangor, Caernarvon, Pwllheli, and Nevin.

---

[3]*Chester.* Vol. XXV. p. 193.

Clusters of villages (usually centred on a parish church or at road junctions), farms, and the houses of the gentry, gave animation to a countryside which contained many lonely stretches where woodland, moor and hillside were more conspicuous than cultivated fields. There were no great centres, and industries were restricted to coal and lead mining in Flintshire and limestone and slate quarrying elsewhere. Trade derived chiefly from the sale of woollens and cattle. The old order of life prevailed in these rural areas and it is doubtful whether the humble countrymen were stirred by the religious and political issues which fanned the flame of fanaticsm in London. When war was declared, loyalty to the squire probably was more potent than fealty to a remote king. It took several years' strife and the sight of Parliamentary raiding parties driving off flocks and herds to arouse real passion and full realization of the grim horrors of war.

During the early stages of the Civil War, Welsh activity centred on the border fortress towns of Chester and Shrewsbury. The levies of Flint and Denbigh counties frequently fought on Cheshire or Shropshire battlefields. Gradual incursions from across the border caused apprehension in Royalist circles, particularly after the Parliamentarian triumph at Marston Moor. When, after Lord Byron's defeat at the battle of Montgomery in September 1644, the Puritan party became more confident, the whole aspect of the war altered and North Wales Cavaliers began to adopt an attitude of defence. The campaign in South Wales bore little relation to that in the North.

It was the protracted siege of Chester which had the greatest influence on affairs in North Wales. Though Denbighshire and Flintshire had experienced an ever-increasing number of raids by Parliamentarians engaged in the siege, it was only after 'the Loyal City' capitulated in February 1646, that a wholesale Parliamentary advance was undertaken.

The petitions sent to the king in Yorkshire before the outbreak of hostilities indicate that—thanks to the inspiration of Richard Lloyd, the king's attorney general for North Wales—the gentry were pledged to support the royal cause and were already making their preparations. The squires who supplied the Deputy Lieutenants, the Justices of the Peace, and the Commissioners of Array, fired by patriotic ardour, laboured to provide Charles with money, munitions and men. It is doubtful whether one of them foresaw to what interminable length the war was to drag its dreary way.

After this lapse of time it is impossible to comprehend the extent to which the passions of the participants were stirred by their conflicting religious convictions. Yet some diluted sentiment has survived, sufficient to cause many persons to range themselves with one side or the other. The Royalist sees Parliamentarians as rebels, knaves and hypocrites; the Puritan considers the king's party cruel, profligate and irreligious.

The obvious truth is that there were good and bad in both camps. In both armies were to be found the scum of humanity which war so frequently brings to the surface, and their evil deeds live after them. There were also high-souled gentlemen who, while abhorring the task of slaying fellow-countrymen, believed so vehemently in the cause they espoused that they gave their wealth and risked their lives to uphold that which they held to be right. For this war differed from those fought for revenge, or gain, or the lust of power, inasmuch as each side strove for an ideal; the one upholding the Crown and the Church, the other struggling for individual freedom and religious liberty.

It seemed a clear-cut issue at the start. As the months passed the war-skein became so entangled that not even the leaders could perceive what pattern was likely to emerge. The Scots took first one side and then the other. Presbyterians strove with Anglicans and then turned aside to clash with Independents. Republicans, Levellers, and Fifth Monarchy Men contributed to the confusion, and in the end the Parliament had to contend with the army which it had created. If some men stumbled is it to be wondered at? Verily they saw through a glass darkly.

To men of simple faith the issue was less involved. Sir Thomas Salusbury asserted that he could not serve the Lord unless he served 'the Lord's annointed.' His kinsman, Colonel William Salesbury, when he learnt that despite his gallant resistence, Denbigh Castle was doomed, could write: 'For the condition of our king and his kingdoms, if God has soe disposed, blessed be his name and welcome be his will.'

The occupation of churches was not always wanton desecration; it must, at times, have been a military necessity. Royalists attacking Nantwich turned Acton Church into a fort. If, as tradition has it, Mytton stabled his horses in Llangwstenin (old) church, it might have been because the weather was inclement and no other shelter was available. The worst sin the Parliamentarians committed at Northop was, apparently, to steal the curate's surplice. Captain Harry Birch at the time of the Brereton raid in Nov., 1643, wrote: 'I myself coming into the church of Hawarden the morning after they were there, found the Common Prayer-Book scattered up and down the chancel, and some well read man, without doubt, conceiving that the Common Prayers had been in the beginning of a poor innocent old church bible, tore out almost all Genesis . . . . In windows where there was oriental glass they broke in pieces only the faces . . . . They had pulled the rails down about the table, and very honestly reared them to the wall (it was well they were in a coal country, where fuel was plentiful) and brought down the table to the midst of the church.' [4]

To the Puritans a table placed against the east wall of the chancel represented an 'altar': hence this gesture of disapprobation.

At variance with the popular conception of iconoclastic Roundheads is the sentiment expressed by a certain 'S.R.' who wrote from Caernarvon on the day after its governor, Lord Byron, surrendered to Major-General Mytton.

'I must tell you they are here, for the matter of religion, most ignorant and brutish people, who know very little of

---

[4] *Phillips.* Vol. 2. p. 114.

God; and it is heartily to be wished that some honest and godly-painful ministers would come to preach the Gospel to them. Indeed, there are some prelates and prelatical clergy in Carnarvon very malignant, and such as the people are like to profit little by, except they will study to preach Jesus Christ more than, for ought I can hear, they have done. The country-towns hereabouts have been quite without all manner of preaching almost. But blessed be God, we are in a fair way to reduce these parts to the obedience of the Parliament who, I doubt not, will take care to send a powerful ministry so soon as North Wales is totally reduced.' [5]

The victors regarded the task of evangelising the vanquished as a serious obligation. In 1649 they formed a Commission for the Propagation of the Gospel in Wales, a body which functioned actively if not always happily for a number of years. Its members included supporters with commissions prominent in less peaceful circles; names which strike a note of irony.

Professor A. H. Dodd writes: 'Until it received its *coup de grâce* in 1653 the Propagation remained the real government of Wales.' [6]

By practical demonstration preachers like Vavasour Powell proved they could wield the broadsword as effectively as the sword of the spirit. Vavasour was wounded in the attack on Beaumaris in 1648. Others like Cornet Jeffrey Parry of Rhydolion were ready to go to prison for their religious convictions. Wrexham district produced a number of earnest Puritans. Many were undoubtedly influenced by Morgan Llwyd the preacher-mystic. Among the men who prayed as well as fought were Captain William Wynne, a commissioner under the Act for the better propagation and preaching of the Gospel in Wales, Captain Gerald Barbour a friend of the Rev. Philip Henry who described him as a 'saint of the Lord', and the valiant Captain Edward Taylor of Pickhill who unhorsed the redoubtable Sir John Owen. Wrexham, in fact, proved to be (in Dr. Thomas Richards'

---

[5]*Phillips.* Vol. 2. p. 309.
[6]*Studies in Stuart Wales.* p. 148.

words) a hotbed of Puritanism and 'bred a numerous crop of cornets and captains.'[7]

Such is the complicated composition of the human personality that saints and sinners intermingled on the Propagation of the Gospel Committee. Here are the names of some who served in North Wales:

COLONEL JOHN JONES, the regicide
SIR JOHN TREVOR, Bart.
CAPTAIN RICHARD PRICE
COLONEL GEORGE TWISTLETON
COLONEL JOHN CARTER
LIEUT.-COLONEL THOMAS MASON
CAPTAIN THOMAS BALL
CAPTAIN HUGH COURTNEY
CAPTAIN EDWARD TAYLOR
CAPTAIN ROGER SONTLEY
CAPTAIN WILLIAM WYNNE
CAPTAIN LUKE LLOYD
CAPTAIN ANDREW ELLIS (who was married to the daughter of Lord Saye and Seele)[8]

An incongruous convocation to spread abroad the doctrine of the Prince of Peace!

[7]Flints. H.S. *Publ.* No. 13. p. 53.
[8]*Studies in Stuart Wales.* p. 152.

CHAPTER TWO

DURING the Civil War there was a complete lack of uniformity of apparel until the formation of the New Model army by the Parliament in 1645. Foot soldiers then adopted the red tunic which was ever after to be the hallmark of the British infantryman. Even so, the colour of their breeches was not specified provided the garments were grey or a similar 'sad' colour. Surprisingly few relics of the arms and armour have survived in this area. While the Office of Works were restoring Conway Castle in 1955 several cannon-balls of small calibre were found.[9] They were probably fired by Parliamentary batteries during the siege of 1646. In the Grosvenor Museum, Chester, is a jack-boot the leather of which is of a thickness which makes one marvel it was ever worn. Several basket-hilted broad-swords are doubtless souvenirs of the fight on Rowton Moor.

Armour was favoured for a short time at the outbreak of hostilities. Gradually it fell into disuse, men preferring to risk wounds rather than suffer the discomfort its wearing entailed. Headpieces were unbearably heavy and were often replaced by broad-brimmed hats. The term 'helmet' was never used. 'Headpiece' was the accepted term though this was usually abbreviated to 'pot'. A cuirass was alluded to as a 'breast-and-back'. Buff-coats were favoured by the cavalry, the thick leather being expected to turn a sword cut. They were usually sleeveless to give the sword arm greater freedom, thus permitting the doublet's sleeves to be seen. Fighting units were divided into four main groups: horse, dragoons, foot, and ordnance.

Mounted men were termed 'horse'. As the senior branch the troopers were well paid (when paid) and better equipped than the foot. They played the determining part in an action which was usually settled by a cavalry charge. The chief weapon was the broadsword. Holster-pistols and carbines were sometimes carried but their use does not seem to have been encouraged. Occasionally a small poll-axe was favoured

---

[9]More have since been discovered in the castle well.

by the Cavaliers. The normal unit was a troop of 120. A trooper provided his own mount on the understanding that he was recompensed in the event of its death or injury.

The title 'dragoon' has changed with the passing years. Then it signified mounted infantry. The men were trained to fight as foot, were armed with muskets, and used their nags (an animal inferior to the cavalry charger) merely as a means of transport.

The rough nature of much of the North Wales terrain made mounted infantry desirable. Sir Richard Lloyd of Esclus commanded a dragoon regiment, Sir Thomas Hanmer of Hanmer raised two companies of dragoons, and Lieutenant-Colonel Thomas Davies of Gwysaney was ordered to combine dragoons with infantry in his regiment of 500 Flintshire men.

Referred to as 'foot', the infantry were divided into two groups: pikemen, who wore protective armour and carried pikes of 16 or 18 foot length; and musketeers, termed 'shot.' At the start the latter were equipped with the cumbersome matchlock which had to be supported on a rest and fired by the application of a smouldering 'match'. The cord of this, several feet in length, was held between the second, third and fourth fingers of the left hand. At night the glow betrayed movements as did the rattle of cartridge-cases which swung from the bandoleers. Risk of explosion was great. The matchlock was replaced by the flintlock as speedily as possible. The ball used weighed an ounce; some were as heavy as 12 to the pound.

Sir Charles Firth[10] quotes Lupton as placing the effective range at 400 yards, but comments: 'the musket was effective at a longer distance than was generally supposed'. Firing was inaccurate. When Nantwich experienced a night attack by Lord Capell's forces several hours' shooting resulted in the death of one calf.

Field-pieces were used in many battles but they did not play an important part except in siege warfare. Siege-pieces such as cannon and culverin required a large team of oxen

---

[10]*Cromwell's Army.* p. 89.

and could only be moved when the road surface was dry. There was no standard of calibre; the weight of shot was approximate. A cannon-ball was usually termed a bullet. The names of ordnance sound strange:

CULVERIN: 18 to 20 lb.
DEMI-CULVERIN: 9 to 10 lb.
SAKER: 6 lb.
MINION: 3½ lb.
DRAKE: 3 lb. or less.
FALCONET: 2 lb.
ROBINET: 1 lb.

In the grounds of Gloddaeth Hall lies an ancient cannon pitted with rust. It is seven feet long and has a bore of 5½ inches—a culverin's measurement. How it came there is a mystery but it was probably used for battering Conway in 1646. Raised ground at Llandudno Junction facing the castle still goes by the name of Cae Battery (Battery Field). Stone balls fired from mortars during the siege have been unearthed at Denbigh and Chester. 'The heaviest piece habitually used in the field was the culverin,' writes Sir Charles Firth. It 'carried point blank about 400 paces, and had an extreme range of 2,100[11] paces. It required eight horses to draw it.'[12]

An infantry regiment was normally 1,200 strong; a dragoon regiment 1,000, but the figures were governed by circumstances. Though Colonel Roger Mostyn raised 1,500 men for the king at the outbreak of war, by 1644 his numbers had dwindled to 300.

'After a few months fighting,' comments Sir Charles Firth, 'the Royalist army was full of colonels whose regiments were no stronger than a troop or a company.'[13]

When a regiment sustained heavy losses it was the king's practice instead of bringing it up to strength to issue a new commission to another colonel to form a fresh regiment.

[11]Rev. William Harrison, *Elizabeth arms England*. (1587) gives the range at 4,000 yards.
[12]*Cromwell's Army*, p. 150.
[13]Ibid. p. 26.

Regiments bore no number but went by their colonel's name. Frequently they wore his colours. Thus, Sir Thomas Fairfax's soldiers had a blue uniform, so had Prince Rupert's Bluecoats. There were also the King's Red Regiment and the Duke of Newcastle's Whitecoats. John Hampden's men wore green.[14] The Earl of Essex's regiment had orange, and this shade, in compliment to the commander-in-chief, was adopted by the Parliament as their badge. Each company carried its own colours to assist in rallying its men during the fog of battle smoke. The old practice of a regiment using its colonel's livery on its facings, and being known by his name, is perpetuated in the Green Howards. Payment of the fighting men was notoriously irregular. The Parliament, with London's financial resources at their disposal, were more consistent in their payments but the result was far from satisfactory. Once General Mytton's own men opened fire on him at Wrexham because they were exasperated at their pay being sadly in arrears. Brereton complained that the Lancashire horse were unreasonable and would not fight unless properly paid.

A document in the Chirk Castle collection throws light on the payments made to the garrison in 1646 after the Royalists had forsaken their trust and Myddelton had regained his majestic home. Infantry, stationed at Chirk, received: lieutenant 14s. per week, ensign (second lieutenant) 10s. 6d, sergeant 5s. 3d., corporal and drummer 3s.[15] This is considerably less than the standard rate quoted by Sir Charles Firth in *Cromwell's Army* which places a lieutenant of foot at 4s. a day and an ensign at 3s.[16] In the instance of the garrison a deduction might, of course, have been made for subsistence. But rates of pay varied.

One of the vexed questions of the war was how troops could be paid. Charles's debt to his amateur soldiers is too great to be computed. Squires like Roger Mostyn, William Price, William Wynne of Melai, Hugh Wynne of Bodysgallen are known to have raised their own regiments at their own

[14]*Oliver Cromwell.* John Buchan. p. 153.
[15]*Mahler.* p. 180.
[16]*Cromwell's Army.* p. 188.

expense and it is quite probable that most of the other gentry also bore the cost even though the fact has not been recorded. When such professional soldiers as Sir John Owen, Colonel Robert Ellice or Lieutenant-Colonel Thomas Davies were ordered to form regiments, it is possible that payment came from the royal war-chest. As time passed and this source became depleted, non-payment of the wages of royalist soldiers (despite levies on various counties and towns, and 'free quartering') caused increasing dissatisfaction, and doubtless was the indirect cause of much of the plundering. It will be noticed that when Chirk Castle was captured, the king ordered Colonel Ellice to dispose of the plunder to provide funds for the new regiment of foot he was to raise. After the Anglesey rebellion of 1648 the gentry responsible for the disturbance were fined a sum sufficient to cover the wages of the officers and common soldiers who had to be called out to suppress it.

'Free quarter' is now little more than an empty phrase. During the Civil War it carried an ominous ring. Householders were compelled to board soldiers on the promise of future payment. Sir Charles Firth writes : 'It did not mean that food and lodging was provided gratis, but that payment for them was deferred.' [17]

War-calloused warriors who did not trouble to differentiate between friend and foe proved unwelcome guests. The bitterness engendered may be imagined.

In piecing together the story of the early years of the war it is inevitable that the emphasis rests on the King's party. The Cavaliers were, in the first place, the dominant party. Records of their activities, such as their petition to Charles at York, have survived to testify to their ardour. Much of the correspondence which has been preserved comes from Royalist pens—possibly because the other writers considered it safer to commit their recorded opinions to the flames. An impression is thus created that the squirarchy of North Wales were Royalists almost to a man, but this was not the case. In South Caernarvonshire men like Thomas Madryn (the sheriff), Thomas Glynne of Glyn-

---

[17]*Cromwell's Army.* p. 218.

llifon, John Bodwrda, William Lloyd of Plashen (who later gave his life for the Parliamentary cause), and even Sir William Williams of Vaenol, had leanings towards the Puritan party but, their habitations being set in a Royalist neighbourhood, they were compelled by circumstances to become Commissioners of Array. In east Denbighshire the Parliament's supporters were not all drawn from the ranks of yeomen farmers and prosperous tradesmen. One of the Broughtons of Marchwiel is said to have strayed from the Royal path followed by so many of his kindred. Major Francis Manley of Erbistock, wounded fighting for the King, had a younger brother, John, who became a major in the opposite camp and acquired considerable influence. Strangest of all, the King's most doughty warrior, Colonel William Salesbury, had as his heir, Captain Owen Salesbury, who fought for the Parliament; an apostasy his stubborn parent never forgave. They died unreconciled.

The conduct of the troops changed as the struggle intensified. There is no indication of cruelty at the start; and not a great deal of disorderliness. In fact, when, during the winter of 1642-3, the troops of Colonel Roger Mostyn got out of hand and looted the Chester house of the Parliamentary commander, the civic authorities were so shocked by this unseemly behaviour that they endeavoured to make restitution. Three years later the event would probably not have elicited comment. The character of the earliest troops was doubtless reflected in their conduct. The soldiers would be mainly volunteers inspired by a principle or stimulated by desire for adventure, or else they were men whose masters required such service. Later, when the supply of volunteers failed to swell the ranks adequately on either side, both parties resorted to conscription. So involved did the war become that it is said that many of the best infantry in the New Model Army were ex-Royalist foot who had obtained their freedom by undertaking to serve their new masters, a decision made easier by the promise of attractive pay.

Idealism, indeed, appears to have been one of the first casualties in this conflict which was ostensibly fought for an ideal.

CHAPTER THREE

1642

To obtain a correct background for the events of the Civil War it is necessary to bear in mind two military occasions which absorbed public attention during 1639 and 1641. First came Charles's futile and humiliating expeditions against the Scots. One benefit indubitably accrued! The mismanagement of the campaigns brought home the unpleasant truth that English amateurs after so many years of peace were ill-prepared for military adventures. The campaigns, however, served the purpose of a dress rehearsal as organisation was necessary to call out the militia.

The general of horse who commanded at Newcastle was no other than Lord Conway, owner of Conway Castle, that nebulous personage who hovers like a spectre over the more material figures of Archbishop Williams and John Owen. Later Lord Conway was transferred to Ireland as general of horse but was recalled to London where he watched the king's interests in the House of Lords. He was prime mover in a conspiracy to raise London for the royal cause, and on its discovery was placed in durance by the Parliament.

Charles, in a letter to Archbishop Williams, explained that Lord Conway could not fortify and provision Conway Castle 'being imprisoned by some of our rebellious subjects.'[18]

In the late autumn of 1641 the country was horrified by news of massacres of Protestants in Ireland. Already regiments had been serving in that country under Lord Strafford's rule, but the Parliament resolved to dispatch in addition 10,000 foot and 2,000 horse to put down the revolt. Once war broke out in England they became a forgotten army until their reappearance tipped the scale in the king's favour. The opportune arrival of the fleet bearing these ragged veterans had a decisive effect on the issue in North Wales.

---

[18]*Hacket*, quoted by Williams, *Aberconwy*, p. 57.

During the summer of 1642 the rumblings of the coming storm grew ominous. King Charles had quitted intransigent London for Yorkshire. After the Scottish campaign the arms of the disbanded militia were stored in the fortress-port of Hull. The king, desirous of securing these to arm his volunteers, rode at the head of 300 Cavaliers to demand their surrender. The governor, Sir John Hotham, shut the city gates in the royal face. Frustrated and humiliated, the Stuart was forced to withdraw. The incident had far-reaching consequences. Had the royal infantry been suitably equipped at Edgehill they would have given a better account of themselves and hundreds of ill-armed Welshmen would have survived the slaughter.

The king was wroth. So, too, was Archbishop Williams in his palace at Cawood.[19] He expressed his opinion of Sir John so vehemently that Hotham's son, when it came to his ears, drew his sword and swore to cut off the prelate's head. When the Archbishop learned that young Hotham had ridden forth to execute his threat, he abandoned Cawood Castle and fled incontinently back to his native town of Conway. As it transpired his unpremeditated act enabled him to serve the royal cause far more effectively than he could have done in Yorkshire.

In North Wales the leading Royalists—inspired by Richard Lloyd of Esclus—penned petitions to the king professing their loyalty and imploring his Majesty to take up arms against the Parliamentary disturbers of the peace.

The Flintshire petition, which bore the signature of the octogenarian knight, Sir Roger Mostyn, was presented to the king at York on August 4. As this was only a matter of three weeks before the king raised his standard at Nottingham, it may be assumed the gentry of North Wales were in active preparation for the approaching conflict.

Wrexham was the largest town in North Wales. Unlike its neighbouring boroughs it possessed no tutelary castle but lay open and exposed. Nevertheless, it was regarded as a convenient centre for assemblies. Only a few miles away

---

[19]Near Selby, Yorkshire.

24

Holt bridge led to the Puritan stronghold, Nantwich, the proximity of which possibly accounted for the strong Parliamentary sentiment which stubbornly persisted in this district.

It was Wrexham which was selected for the meeting of the gentry of Denbighshire and Flintshire that August when they unanimously resolved to raise a regiment of volunteers for the king, and to subscribe £1,500 for the purpose. For the commanding officer they chose Sir Thomas Salusbury, second baronet of Lleweni, the paramount house of West Denbighshire. A comparatively young married man, with a son eight years old, Sir Thomas had served in the Short Parliament but was better known as an Oxford scholar, with a predilection for poetry. From a letter he wrote at the time it is obvious he was an idealist who regarded the campaign as tantamount to a crusade to uphold the divine right of kings.

According to Judge Bulstrode Whitelock young Roger Mostyn raised 1,500 men for the king in 12 hours. If this applies to a separate regiment it signifies that these two counties alone contributed over two thousand of the Welshmen who followed the king to Edgehill.

In Caernarvonshire Colonel John Owen, who returned to his native county to recruit a regiment of volunteers, met with less response, and could not muster sufficient men to join in the march from Shrewsbury which ended at Edgehill. And this despite the lure that the regiment would form a life-guard for the Prince of Wales, the saturnine twelve-year-old destined to attain notoriety as the Merrie Monarch.

When the king sojourned at Shrewsbury he presented to the town two pieces of ordnance for its defence. Considering these insufficient, the Shrewsbury Royalists applied to the king for his good offices with the gentlemen of Caernarvonshire to procure them the loan of additional artillery. On December 31 his Majesty at Oxford addressed a letter to John Griffith esq., and others of that county desiring them to lend him 'such pieces of artillery as may be of use to our towne of Shrewsbury; undertaking to return them att the end of the service, unless in the interim it shall be agreed

The Burgesse's Tower,
Denbigh.

THE BURGESS GATE

*The principal entrance to the Old Town of Denbigh still stands
but is partly obscured by houses*

between you and the said towne to buy and sell the said peeces.' [20]

Many cart-loads of arms were brought to Shrewsbury out of Flintshire and Denbighshire.[21]

King Charles visited North Wales on several occasions. In 1645 he slept at Chirk Castle and also at Denbigh Castle. He was twice at Wrexham. On September 27, 1642, he addressed the populace from the old shire hall—later burnt. On October 7, he returned and was the guest at Bryn-y-Ffynnon, the town house of Richard Lloyd, whom he knighted.[22]

Events in North Wales must necessarily have been influenced by the stand taken by the loyal city of Chester. Though there were many changes in the garrison during the war the core appears to have been consistently provided by the regiments of Colonel Hugh Wynne and Colonel Roger Mostyn.

Surprisingly little has been preserved about the part played by North Wales troops in the battle of Edgehill. Charles and his amateur army set forth from Shrewsbury on October 12, intent on capturing London. The Earl of Essex with a larger force marched north to intercept him. So deficient was the scout-craft of both sides that the armies passed each other without being aware of their proximity. Thus, when contact was made, Charles had his back to his capital and Essex faced the city he intended to protect.

It is common knowledge that the king's success was jeopardised by Rupert's irresponsible charge—in which he was followed by Sir John Byron who commanded the reserve of horse. As a result the Royalist foot were left unprotected. For several hours they were at push of pike. The Welsh under Salusbury formed the second line of defence. In the gathering gloom the bewildered, ill-armed men of Flint and Denbigh crowded together to face the flashing broadswords of Balfour's cavalry until, in the chill October twilight, the field was strewn with slashed corpses, soon to be tumbled

[20]Owen and Blakeway. *Hist. of Shrewsbury.* 1. p. 432.
[21]Ibid. p. 429.
[22]D.N.B.

into communal graves. There are no casualty lists. Perhaps those turf tombs account for the absence of some well known North Wales names from the annals of the Civil War. The Welsh unfortunates do not appear to have made a good showing. A Robert Evans, referring to Colonel Salusbury, wrote that his fellow countrymen were '1,200 poor Welsh vermin, the offscowering of the nation.'

It seems clear that Sir Thomas Salusbury was engaged in the battle. The king marched to Oxford which he entered on October 29, and soon after this Sir Thomas was awarded the degree of D.C.L. by the university.[23] This infers that he went there with the king.

A couple of weeks after Edgehill the Welsh infantry of Salusbury's regiment redeemed their reputation. When the king's march on London was checked at Brentford, the barricades which had defied Rupert's horsemen were stormed by the men of Denbighshire—who incidentally plundered the town by way of recompense.

Warburton writes: —

'Rupert soon indulged himself and his favourite regiment, the Prince of Wales' by making a bold dash at Brentford capturing on his way the advanced post at Sir Richard Gwynn's and charging into the streets of Brentford.'[24]

Deterred by the menace of the London trained bands assembled on Turnham Green, the king retired to Oxford and his forces went into winter quarters. The university city, overcrowded, would have no accommodation for soldiers not required to man the defences. Colonel Salusbury's decimated regiment made their way back to the more congenial confines of North Wales.

With Christmas came the hope of compromise. A 'bare and poor truce.' (to quote Archbishop Williams), was arranged in Cheshire but it was short lived. The good prelate

---

[23]D.N.B.
[24]Quoting Clarendon. III 327. This advanced post was probably Sir Richard Wynn's house at "Brainford" at it was termed (Vide. C.W.P.).

regarded the issue lightheartedly at this time for a letter written from his home at Penrhyn shows that he was 'engaged in so many visits and feasts at Tom Bulkeley's [Baron Hill] and Sir William Williams' [Vaenol] that it will be nine, ten or twelve days at the least before he can leave these parts.' [25]

Edgehill survivors must have straggled home with tales of the fight but no written record appears to have been preserved. The rigours of the campaign may have proved too severe for the constitution of the poet-soldier, Sir Thomas Salusbury, for by the following August he was dead. No further reference occurs to the regiment of which he was colonel. At Mostyn Hall is a silver medallion inscribed *R. Mostyn*. According to family tradition it was picked up on the battle-field and is accepted as proof of Roger's presence at Edgehill.

No warlike activity is indicated in North Wales but doubtless the drilling of trained-bands, the manufacture of powder, and the collection of weapons went on under the inspiring leadership of Sir Richard Lloyd, Attorney General for North Wales. His Wrexham home was admirably placed for preserving contact with the loyal fortress towns of Shrewsbury and Chester.

The outstanding organisers for the king at this period were Archbishop Williams in the west and Sir Richard Lloyd in east Denbighshire. Sir Richard evidently found Esclus Hall too remote, for he acquired as his town house the famous Bryn-y-ffynnon which had hitherto belonged to John Jones of Maes-y-garnedd, who later attained questionable fame as 'the regicide'. Whether Sir Richard purchased Bryn-y-ffynnon or took possession under the exigencies of war is uncertain. His tombstone in Wrexham parish church proclaims that he was:

'a loyal and devoted subject and servant of the Royal Martyr, Charles I, whom he received at Bryn-y-Ffynnon in this town in the year 1642.'

---

[25] C.W.P. 1719. *Note*. Charles's letters sent to the Commissioners of Array for Caernarvonshire are printed in full in an appendix to the Rev. P. B. Williams' *Guide to Caernarvonshire*. 1821.

Charles's first visit to Wrexham on September 27 during his journey from Chester to Shrewsbury must have been a memorable occasion. High Street would doubtless be packed with people. According to tradition the king addressed the inhabitants of the counties of Denbigh and Flint from a window of the ancient Shire Hall.

It is apparent that by this time the local volunteers had reached Shrewsbury. This is implied in Charles's opening words.

'I am willing to take all occasions to visit all my good subjects, in which number I have cause to reckon you of these two counties, and having lately had a good expression of your loyalty and affection to me by those levies, which at your charge have been sent me from your part (which forwardness of yours I shall always remember to your advantage) and to let you know how I have been dealt with by a powerful malignant party in this Kingdom, whose designs are no less than to destroy my person and crown, the laws of the land, and the present government both of Church and State.'

After denouncing the subtlety and cunning practices of the Parliamentary leaders the King continued:

'I am robbed and spoiled of my towns, forts, castles, and goods; my navy forcibly taken from me and employed against me; all my revenue stopped and seized upon; and at this time a powerful army is marching against me. I wish this were all. They have yet laboured further to alienate the affections of my good people.'

Charles concluded:

'My confidence is in the protection of Almighty God and the affections of my good people. And that you may clearly see what my resolutions are I shall cause my voluntary protestation lately taken, to be read to you. And I desire that the Sheriffs of these two counties will dispose copies of that, and what I now deliver unto you, having no other way to make it public.' *

In an atmosphere of uncertainty and anxiety the good folk of North Wales waited to see what the new year would bring forth.

---

*Printed in full in Phillips vol. 2., pp. 20-22.

CHAPTER FOUR

1643

THE dawn of 1643 saw the people of North Wales looking outward over the invisible wall of the border, less concerned with domestic affairs than in devising support for the cause in England. It was not until autumn that the seriousness of the conflict was realized. The first and obvious centre of their interest was Chester. Lying a matter of twelve miles from Wrexham where Royalist manor-houses clustered thickly it would be the first citadel to which the king's supporters would gravitate, even as it was the Mecca of the Mostyns, the Whitleys, and Pennants dwelling nearer the coast. From the outset the names of Hugh Wynne, Roger Mostyn and Robert Ellice were associated with Chester, the outworks of which were planned by Ellice. Welshmen comprised a large proportion of the garrison. The good people of Shropshire, however, had some claim and they wrote to the Denbighshire Commissioners pointing out that Salop was 'their guard from any force of the Parliament,' and suggested that North Wales contributed something to the cause. Accordingly Colonel William Wynne of Melai (near Llangernyw) marched his regiment to support Lord Capell in Shropshire, while Major Robert Broughton of Marchwiel offered his services to Sir Michael Woodhouse who acted as Capell's sergeant-major-general of foot. As the months passed the interest of Colonel Ellice and Sir Richard Lloyd centred more on Shrewsbury than Chester, doubtless because that town was nearer the seat of war. The appointment of Prince Rupert as President of Wales and commander-in-chief of the area would have been an undoubted attraction, particularly when his Highness chose Shrewsbury for his headquarters during his ephemeral command.

Charles ordered Colonel Ellice to capture Chirk Castle. This was accomplished with apparent ease, Myddelton being absent in London. His steward, Watkin Kyffin, was taken prisoner. William Maurice records:

> 1643. 15th of January: Chirk Castle taken and plundered by Colonell Ellis.

The loss of this important stronghold was as big a reverse to the Parliamentarians as it was a great gain to the King's party. Sir Thomas Hanmer was appointed governor for a short while but he was soon succeeded by Colonel John Watts.

In January 1643 Sir Francis Ottley was appointed governor of Shrewsbury and he kept in close touch with the leading men of North Wales. Shropshire was without Parliamentary opposition until the Puritan party established a headquarters at the open market town of Wem which they proceeded to fortify. The command was conferred upon Colonel Thomas Mytton of Halston, thereby introducing a soldier who was destined to play a conspicuous part in the affairs of North Wales.

In Cheshire the Parliamentarians, led by Sir William Brereton, a baronet of ancient lineage, encircled Nantwich 'round aboute with Stronge Trenches & mudwalls of Clodds & Earthe',[26] and adopted this town as their headquarters. The principal posts along the Severn were in Royalists' hands and barge-loads of munitions and provisions freely passed along this watery highway. The crossings of the Dee were watched by garrisons at Holt, Overton, and Bangor-is-y-Coed. Denbighshire provided 400 musketeers for the purpose.[27] Well might the good people of North Wales consider themselves secure.

The loyalist baronet, Sir Thomas Aston, sallied from Chester intent on capturing Nantwich before the defence works were completed but he sustained a severe defeat by Brereton on January 28.

On February 2, Colonel Mostyn's Welsh soldiers got out of hand in Chester and sacked The Nunnery, the town

---

[26] *Hall.* p. 147.
[27] Prof. A. H. Dodd. D.H.S. *Tr.* vol. III, p. 53.

house of Sir William Brereton, smashing windows, stripping off lead and carrying away furniture and goods. City officials interfered and endeavoured to restore what property they could but Brereton cherished resentment. It is probable that the tenacity of his siege was not unconnected with this incident. Sir Thomas Aston set forth again on March 11 resolved to redeem his lost reputation by an attack on Middlewich. Colonel Robert Ellice accompanied him with his Welsh regiment. In a night engagement Aston was again worsted, and Colonel Ellice was taken and marched captive to Manchester. Major Gilmore and some 600 infantrymen were among the prisoners. Ellice was exchanged in September. With him were imprisoned 'Captyn Johnes, Captyn Morrys and Captyn Eaton.' [28]

In April 1643, Prince Rupert 'entered and possessed the seditious town of Birmingham, wherein was 300 Foot and two Troops of Horse, who being gallantly charged by the Welsh-men, in less than half an hour forsook their Breastwork and retired to the Barracadoes within the Town.' [29]

That summer a party of Parliamentarians from Nantwich embarked on a nocturnal attack on the house of Sir Thomas Hanmer, in Flintshire, hoping to surprise it. They were ambushed by Welsh soldiers led by Sir Richard Willis, Capell's major-general of horse, and driven back with heavy losses.

The sale of cattle and Welsh cottons—a name applied to a coarse woollen fabric—was seriously affected by the hostilities and the inhabitants of North Wales petitioned the king for safe conduct for the clothiers and drovers to allow them to pass safely through his Majesty's army. The petition bore the signatures of Colonel Thomas Madryn, sheriff of Caernarvonshire, Rowland Vaughan, sheriff of Merionethshire, Sir William Williams, Colonel Richard Bulkeley, William Hookes, Owen Wynn of Gwydir and other leading men. [30]

The cattle trade was considerable and, in the words of

[28] *Hall.* p. 147.
[29] *Mercurius Belcicus.*
[30] *C.W.P.* 1724.

Archbishop Williams represented 'the Spanish fleet of North Wales which brings hither that little gold and silver we have.' [31]

When Rupert demanded money, the archbishop contended that it was pointless for the soldiers to clamour for wages when the country had no money with which to pay them owing to there being no free sale of cattle. Wales was not merely called upon for men and money, there was an insatiable demand for powder and weapons. While worthy Thomas Bushell melted down family plate at the royal mint in Shrewsbury others laboured to provide more substantial support. Gunsmiths were rounded up and concentrated in the fortress town where a vigilant eye saw that the pistols, muskets and carbines they manufactured did not find their way into enemy hands.

The Calendar of Wynn Papers records that in the summer of 1643, Robert Dolben of Denbigh was commanded to wait on the Commissioners of Array at Ruthin to arrange for his protection while he manufactured gunpowder in North Wales. He was to undertake the work at his own expense but the commissioners allowed him to dig 'all their houses for the making of salt-petre', but he was 'to leave all floors as he found them, and to offer the powder as cheap as he can afford.' [32]

This letter (written to Owen Wynn at Gwydir) imparts the information that there were many Parliamentary ships in Chester Water (the Dee estuary) intending to land at Flint.

A far-reaching move that year was the Parliament's commissioning on June 12 of Sir Thomas Myddelton of Chirk to be their sergeant-major-general for the six North Wales counties, to wage war against 'many Papists, notorious delinquents, and other ill-affected persons.' Despite his age Sir Thomas proved himself a capable general and had a number of successful enterprises to his credit before the Self-Denying Ordinance relieved him of his command. On August 10 Myddelton marched north from London with

[31]Ibid 1748
[32]Ibid 1723.

forces which included seven large guns, four 'cases of drakes', and forty carriages of ammunition.

Welsh troops must have participated in many incidents of which there is no record. For instance, the *Ottley Papers*[33] show there were Welsh soldiers accompanying Lord Capell when he marched to relieve Warrington only to find that the town had surrendered. As he retired to Whitchurch an attempt was made to ambush him in 'a woody ground'. The Parliamentarians, with a party of horse attending them, were 'repulsed by our Welsh without any loss to us, or them, for all we came to knowe.'

Colonel John Owen had succeeded in getting his regiment together and led them south to where Prince Rupert was besieging Bristol. A number of Welsh, including Lieutenant-Colonel Thelwall, participated in the assault, during which Colonel Owen was severely wounded in the throat. The letter he wrote to his wife describing the mishap is extant.[34] He survived and returned to North Wales with dramatic results.

One of the leading royalists of the Wrexham district was Sir Edward Broughton, father of the Major Broughton who was wounded at Wem. He dwelt at the Old Hall which lies at no great distance from the Cheshire border. Among Sir Thomas Myddelton's soldiers who were then stationed at Nantwich were local men who were well acquainted with the district. On the morning of October 23, 1643, members of Myddelton's troop, assisted by men of Nantwich companies marched into Wales, and took the Hall by surprise, capturing Sir Edward and two of his sons, all of whom they brought prisoner to Nantwich.[35]

Meanwhile the Royalists in Shropshire were tasting the bitterness of internecine strife. Much of the money subscribed for the local cause had gone to the king at Oxford, and the trained bands were forced to raid the countryside for subsistence.

This atmosphere of Royalist discontent enheartened

---

[33]*O.P.* p. 138.
[34]*Mitre & Musket*, B. Dew Roberts. p. 217.
[35]*Hall.* p. 157.

the Parliamentary party who renewed their efforts to fortify Wem. To give Colonel Mytton the benefit of their experience Sir William Brereton and Sir Thomas Myddelton marched south to superintend the work. Myddelton's Welsh soldiers formed part of the garrison of Nantwich and were probably with the force.[36]

There followed a grim game of hide-and-seek played by men with sword and musket in their hands, for Lord Capell, learning that Brereton had marched towards Wem, surreptitiously assembled an army of between 4,000 and 5,000 men. Moving by night he essayed to capture Nantwich in Brereton's absence. His men reached Acton Church which lies a mile from Nantwich whereupon the town's defenders, despite their depleted numbers, sallied forth to give battle. Here a struggle raged in the churchyard and the invaders were driven to seek shelter in the church. Unable to dislodge them the townspeople returned to the security of their mud walls to await the anticipated assault. Word of their predicament was carried to Brereton who instantly halted his force and hastened back to their aid. Capell was informed of this and, after his men pillaged friend and foe alike, he hurried from Acton resolved to carry out his original plan to attack Wem. The two forces missed each other in the darkness.

When day dawned, Wem's three hundred defenders found themselves facing the advance guard of several thousand royalists. An assault was promptly delivered and a fierce battle followed on that momentous morn of October 18. Here, on the ramparts, Colonel William Wynne of Melai was slain, and his Welsh soldiers, discouraged by the loss of so popular an officer, abandoned the fight. Capell's men withdrew to Shrewsbury, ten miles away, taking with them the corpse of the colonel for interment in St. Chad's church.

Brereton's weary warriors on learning they had missed their foes again set out for Wem, finally refusing to march further until they had rested. The fight was over when they neared Wem but they made a half-hearted attempt to harass

---

[36]Ibid. p. 155.

the retiring Royalists. Both sides were too fatigued to settle the issue. In the assault on Wem the Welsh suffered heavily. Among the wounded were Major Broughton of Marchwiel and Captain Manley of Erbistock. The exulting victors claimed that sixty Royalists were slain by one discharge from 'a case of drakes'. Six carriage-loads of dead were carted from the field and (adds the report) thirty more corpses were left on the ground. This was the worst misfortune so far experienced by the Cavaliers of North Wales. A greater shock was to follow.

Though Royalists had taken Chirk Castle the Myddelton influence was not exterminated. The Commissioners of Array at Chirk experienced difficulty in raising trained bands for the king's service and Kenrick Eyton, John Edwardes and John Trevor, three of the commissioners found it necessary to issue warrants to apprehend those who were backward in enlisting. On the very eve of the Brereton raid Edwardes wrote to Sir Richard Lloyd : 'I have hastened the soldiers you desired, the delay has been caused by the illness of Mr. John Trevor, who could not assist me . . . . I have no arms with which to furnish the men.' [37]

In view of the menace from the Cheshire Parliamentarians the hundred of Bromfield raised 124 musketeers 'to guard the passages upon the river Dee,' and provided £150 to pay them for a month. The commissioners suggested that Chirk might contribute a hundred men and £100 to support them. [38]

Once the weather broke it was customary for troops to go into winter quarters, but Brereton, now reinforced by Myddelton, decided to invade North Wales. On November 7 the combined forces marched out of Nantwich. They moved at a leisurely pace, spending the first night at Woodhey and the second at Barton-on-the-Hill. [39] As they neared Farndon they were joined by some Lancashire men under Colonel John Booth. Though the invasion was, in a sense a surprise, it was not wholly unexpected. Tidings had reached the

[37]*Mahler.* p. 166.
[38]Ibid. 165.
[39]*Hall.* p. 157.

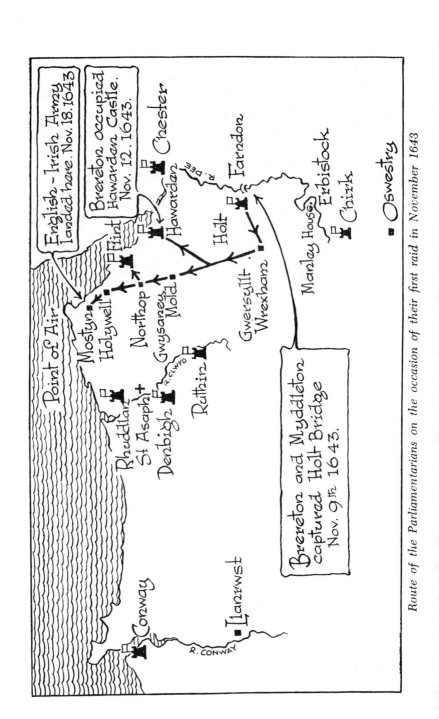

Route of the Parliamentarians on the occasion of their first raid in November 1643

governor at Holt Castle, Lieutenant-Colonel John Robinson, who dispatched a party to cross the river and dispute the enemy's advance. The Welsh bank of the river was lined with musketeers from Colonel Ellice's new regiment, supported by Major Marcus Trevor's regiment of horse. Brereton in his dispatch claimed he had to face 'all the strength and power in Wales.' Numbers might be imposing but it will be seen from Edwardes' letter there was some raw material in the Royalists' ranks. Bells ('rung backwards') and flaring beacons spread an alarum across apprehensive Denbighshire.

At that time Holt bridge possessed a gate-house in the centre. This was protected by a drawbridge and strong gates. No trace remains but the structure is clearly indicated on a plan.[40] Both Royalists and Roundheads considered that it would be 'very difficult if not impossible' to force a passage. The invaders' first attempt was to send a party across the Dee in boats, but they were met by such a fierce fusillade from Ellice's musketeers that they returned to their own bank. A feint was then attempted, a large body of Roundheads marching down river as if they intended to cross elsewhere. While the defenders' attention was distracted a sudden rush for the bridge enabled Brereton's men to place ladders against the gatehouse and cut the ropes of the drawbridge. This fell down, giving access to the gates. Hand 'granadoes' were cast over amongst the Welshmen 'which struck such terror as they all run away.' The gates were forced open and the Royalists beaten from their double works. Brereton wrote that they pursued Colonel Ellice's regiment of foot, Major Trevor's regiment of horse 'and all the forces which could be arranged in the adjoining parts of Wales.' [41]

They took about forty common prisoners, one captain, four or five lieutenants, one cornet, and it was reported that there was a lieutenant-colonel also among the prisoners. 'About six o'clock Thursday evening we entered Wrexham,' wrote Brereton. 'The enimy fly apace and begin to remove

---

[40]Denb. H.S. *Tr.* vol. 4. p. 32.
[41]*Chester.* vol. XXV. pp. 45-46. (quoting Portland MS 151).

all their goodes out of these partes, but Holt Castle holds out, butt is beseidged.' [42]

Thomas Malbon states that the bridge was gained about one o'clock 'throughe a pollicie' without loss of a man. The king's force was supposed to be 1,000 horse and 700 foot. Prisoners sent to Nantwich included 'Captaine Preece, Captyn Johnes and Lieuftent Salusbury.'

'On Thursdaye Nighte, after they had taken Holte & left a considerable ptie theire, They marched to wrixam; where they weire well entertayned & quartered theire that Nighte.' [43]

The following morning Brereton led part of the invading force to Hawarden. Immediately the Roundheads appeared before the royal fortress the gates were opened by Col. Thomas Ravenscroft of Pickhill, member of an old Flintshire family, who was supported by Col. John Aldersey. As Ravenscroft that day borrowed a barrel of gunpowder from Chester the cries of 'treachery' were loud. Colonel John Booth with 900 men stayed in Wrexham. There, too, was Sir Thomas Myddelton who, doubtless encouraged by the fall of Hawarden, wrote to the governor of Denbigh, Col. William Salesbury, summoning him to hand over that castle. It was a friendly missive.

'The former friendship and familiarity wch hath passed betwixt us doth not only invite but also engage me to use all possible means not only to continue but alsoe to encrease the same . . . I doe hereby invite you, and desire God that you may for your own good embrace it, that you would please to submitt yourself to the power and obedience of the king and parliament,[44] lay down your armes, and deliver up that castle to mee . . .' He signed himself: 'Your ould true friend and kinsman.' [45]

---

[42]Ibid. p. 46.
[43]Hall. p. 157.
[44]The expression invariably used by the parliament who contended they did not fight against the king, but for him to preserve him from the evil counsellors who led him astray.
[45]A.&M. p. 214.

But Colonel Salesbury was of different mettle from Colonel Ravenscroft, his son-in-law. His response was courteous but firm:

'But to be playne—to betray soe great a trust as the keeping of Denbigh castle, tho' upon ever soe fayre pretences, may be acceptable to them that desire it, but in my opinion, in itself is abominable.' [46]

There the matter ended. Salesbury (who had recently received his commission from the king) and his relatives restored the castle at their own cost. In Wrexham soldiers sheltered in the parish church where they 'broke in pieces one of the best pair of organs in the King's dominions, which Sir Thomas Myddelton took for proper pillage, to make bullets out of.' [47] Another account states that Brereton went to 'Wrexham, Flint and Holywell, and did pull down the organs, defaced the windows in all the churches, and the monuments of divers, and pulled down all the arms [coats-of-arms] and hatchments.'

From Conway Archbishop Williams complained to Ormonde.

'For now . . . the enemies are possessed of Worrall, where your excellency intended to land, and entered into Denbighshire, have taken Wrexham and Ruthin (as some say), plunder up and down the whole country, without resistance; and whether with a resolution to fortify here, or to return again and besiege Chester upon the Welsh as well as the English side, I am not able to conjecture. So that if the English-Irish army shall now come over, unless it be so well provided (by sea and land) as to force their entertainment in Lancashire, Liverpool (which they now seem to neglect as I am informed), or Worrall, where it is feared they will fortify, they will be necessitated to land somewhere in these parts, or at Holyhead, and so much discommodated by the poverty of the country through which they are to pass, and those two ferries at Beaumaris and

---

[46]*A.&M.* p. 215.
[47]*Phillips*, vol. 2, p. 114.

Conway, which of necessity they are to waft over very incommodiously, and (as far as I can conceive) without carrying their cannon with them, but sending it by sea to meet them at Orme's Head, Abergele, Rhyddlan, or as neare Conway as the enemies' advancing will permit and give them leave. And how I shall be able to keep this town of Conway (without any power of command, but that weak one of kindred and good-will) without any assistance of souldiers or Commissions of Array, is to myself very doubtful.' [48]

Conway Castle at this time was evidently without a garrison for Williams asked Ormonde to send by Captain Bartlett's ship one company of Yorkshiremen or Welshmen. He undertook to provide them with meat, drink, shoes and stockings, provided they came armed with some ammunition for which he would pay. The letter was written on the twelfth; a more pessimistic one followed on the 18th. 'But, alas! we grow daily in more uncertainty of the landing of the forces from your parts than we were,' he wrote, little knowing that the troops from Dublin were even then being rowed ashore at Mostyn. He again appealed for his company of a hundred soldiers but this time he did not specify that they should be Welshmen or Yorkshiremen. 'I do not care of what country they are, so as they come with arms and competency of ammunition.'

An indication of the potential man-power of the area at that time is contained in this letter. If the forces from Ireland landed there, he wrote, 'they shall be waited on by two or three thousand foot at the least, and some two or three hundred horse, to the skirts of England.' [49] The old 'militia' idea had not died out—the prelate knew the men would be reluctant to serve outside North Wales! He also asks that these 'auxiliaries' should be provided with 'arms and ammunition'—the lack of which was a perennial problem to the Commissioners of Array.

From Hawarden Brereton wrote the governor of Chester, Sir Abraham Shipman, calling upon him to

[48]Ibid, pp. 93-94.
[49]Ibid. p. 100.

surrender the city, to which Shipman sent a contemptuous reply that if Brereton desired Chester he must 'win and wear it.'

While Brereton was at Hawarden another force consisting of some 600 horse and foot marched down the road to Mold, and having possessed this town, pressed on towards Holywell and Flint. They could not have reached Flint before November 11, and as they were in retreat on the 18, the so-called siege of the castle must have been of brief duration. A party continued along the coast to Mostyn Hall which they captured, taking four cannon, but before they could remove these pieces, a Royalist fleet of some sixteen vessels dropped anchor off the coast and the invaders turned tail.

The ships bore some 2,500 'English-Irish' (to use Archbishop Williams' term) under Sir Michael Ernley, Major-General Richard Gibson, Sir Francis Butler, Major Edward Hamond and George Wynne. With their landing the whole condition changed. Flint Castle was abandoned.

Brereton forsook Hawarden Castle, leaving a garrison of 120 men to their fate. Colonel Roger Mostyn and Lieutenant-Colonel Thomas Davies who, according to Brereton's dispatch, 'fled', quickly reappeared and led the new-comers to Hawarden which was invested. The Welsh, some 500 strong, took over most of the duties, being augmented by a force from Chester under Lieutenant-Colonel John Robinson of Gwersyllt. The majority of the English-Irish marched into Chester where housewives knitted stockings for the ragged warriors.

Chester was heartily glad of the respite and Lord Byron, who had recently arrived as commander under Lord Capell, was gratified to have so many trained soldiers under his charge.

Captain Thomas Sandford, commanding the firelocks from Ireland, sent a 'big letter' to the garrison at Hawarden —'if you put me to the least trouble or loss of blood to force you, expect no quarter for man, woman or child.'

According to Orlando Bridgman, Hawarden was 'blocked up by 1,000 men, most of them of the country.' The latter would be the Welshmen under Colonel Roger Mostyn and Lieutenant-Colonel Thomas Davies.

The Roundheads in reply to a verbal summons to surrender wrote: 'We fear the loss of our religion more than the loss of our dearest blood.' After an exchange of letters the garrison finally capitulated on December 4. A condition of surrender was that the besieged should be allowed to march away with half their arms, one colour and £25 worth of goods, though, as it transpired, the Parliamentarians were badly treated by 'some of the Lord Cholmley's men.'[50] Colonel Mostyn and Colonel Davies accepted the surrender.

When visualizing incidents at Hawarden Castle it must be borne in mind that the present highway is not older than the start of the last century. The old road ran alongside the east face of the walls, overlooked by the barbican, the entrance, and the portion containing the living quarters. The keep or round tower was on the opposite side.

Brief though the Parliamentary raid was, it caused consternation. Henceforth the Royalists in North Wales had little sense of security. This may well have been the time when they began to deposit their valuables in the strongrooms of the castles.

Sometime about Christmas, Byron assembled 4,000 foot and 1,000 horse with the idea of marching through Cheshire to link up with the Shropshire army under Lord Capell.

In the meanwhile Archbishop Williams at Conway had received a summons from the king to attend the 'parliament' which was to be held at Oxford. It might be well, at this juncture, to look back to see what the prelate had been doing.

Archbishop Williams, after establishing himself at Conway, had proceeded to put the ruined castle in a state of repair, and was encouraged in this self-imposed task by his monarch who, on August 1, 1643, wrote to him from Oxford.

---

[50]*Phillips.* vol. 2. p. 113.

'And whereas you are now resident at our Town of Aber-Conway, where there is a Castle, heretofore belonging to our Crown, and now to the Lord Conway, which with some charge is easily made defensible; but the Lord Conway being imprisoned by some of our rebellious subjects, and not able to furnish it, as is requisite for our service, and the defence of those parts: you having begun at your own Charge to put the same into repair, we do heartily desire you to go on in that Work, assuring you that whatsoever Moneys you shall lay out upon the Fortification of the said Castle, shall be repayed unto you, before the Custody thereof shall be put into any other hand, than your own, or such as you shall recommend.' [51]

The archbishop had undertaken the work with characteristic zeal and thoroughness and, once the Parliamentarians had taken Flint and Hawarden castles, he evidently thought Conway was in jeopardy for he pleaded with Ormonde 'to spare 100 able soldiers, well commanded for officers, for the guard of this strong town and castle, where they shall have good quarters, and be ready at six days' warning to return again to Dublin.' [52]

The threat was of short duration and doubtless the prelate left Conway with an easy mind when, towards the end of December he rode off on the long and dangerous journey which was to carry him to Oxford where Charles had summoned his 'parliament' to meet on January 22, 1643/4.

The archbishop lodged with the Provost of Queen's, and though he was not actually appearing as a member of the convocation, Charles asked for his advice.

He gave it fearlessly. It proved unpalatable though events were to vindicate his judgment. Bishop Hacket records the prelate's words:

'Your militia is courageous, but small, not like to increase, and then not to hold out. Your enemies multiply, and by this time your army hath taught them to fight;

---

[51] *Hacket.*
[52] *Phillips.* vol. 2. p. 100.

they are in treaty with the Scots to make a recruit; and the Princes and States beyond the seas, to their shame, give them countenance. Their treasurers at Westminster boast that it costs them large moneys every month to keep Correspondence with their intelligencers and spies about you. Your soldiers in their march and quarters are very unruly, and lose the people's affection everywhere.

'Out of these premises, I infer and engage my life to your Majesty's justice and my soul to God's tribunal that I know no better course than to struggle no further, since it is the will of God, and to refer all to the pleasure and discretion of that unkind and insolent Parliament at Westminster, but with the preservation of your Majesty's Crown and Person, to which they have all taken an oath to offer no hurt or violence .... But if your Majesty disdain to go so low, I am ready to run on in the common hazard with your Majesty, and to live and die in your service.'

Rupert and the hot-heads who followed him, all of whom anticipated an easy victory, were indignant, and it might well be that from this moment Rupert was prejudiced against the prelate. The decision to appoint Sir John Owen as governor of Conway probably had its birth at this time.

Despite the risk from Parliamentary armies the archbishop 'by easy journeys' returned safely to Conway. Williams was at Worcester on May 6 and by the 19 he wrote from Conway: 'I am once more come to these partes'. It was, says Ambrose Philips, 'the last journey of his life'.

While he was absent the fighting round about the Cheshire border had undergone a complete change. Lord Byron, elated at being reinforced by the veteran regiments from Ireland, took the offensive. The newcomers had seen rough service during their campaign and a cruelty, hitherto not noticeable, intruded. At the little village of Barthomley, some twenty villagers who had sought safety in the church were smoked out and cut to pieces.[53]

---

[53]*Hall.* p. 159.

The officer of the English-Irish soldiers, Major Con-naught, granted the suffocating villagers quarter if they came out. 'But,' wrote Malbon, 'when hee had theim in his power, hee caused theim all to be stripped starke Naked; And moste barboriouslie & contr'y to the Lawes of Armes, murthered, stabbed and cutt the Throats of xij of theim.'*

The Parliamentary cause was struck a shrewd blow by the loss of Beeston Castle on its towering crag. Malbon writes:

'On Wednesday morninge, the xiij of December 1643, a litle before Daye, and after the Moon was sett, Captyn Sandford wᵗʰ viij of his fyerlocks, gott into the vpper warde of Beeston Castle, by a byeway, throughe treachery, as was supposed. For a litle after hee was entered, Thomas Steele, then gou'nor of the said Castle, after a shorte ply [parley] betwixt theim, Receyved Sandford into his Lodginge in the Lower warde, where they Dyned together, & much Beere was sente up into the heigher warde, by the said Steele vnto Sandfords soldyeʳˢ.'

As a result the sixty men of the garrison marched out with colours flying and Beeston became a King's castle. For his betrayal Captain Steele was shot behind Nantwich Church.

It was during this December of 1643 that Simon Thelwall, Member of Parliament for Denbigh borough, chose to make his journey to Pembrokeshire. He was a son of the famous house of Plas-y-Ward, near Ruthin. Though his kinsmen served the king, Simon, who was 41 when war broke out, followed the lead of Sir Thomas Myddelton. It has been suggested that the arrival of the English-Irish caused Thelwall to 'cut for his life', but the excellence of his long dispatch to the Parliament, with his detailed and lucid

---

*Lord Byron on December 26, wrote to Lord Newcastle: "The Rebels possessed themselves of a Church at Bartomley, but wee presently beat them forth of it, and put them all to the sword, which I find to be the best way to proceed with their kind of people, for mercy to them is cruelty." The letter fell into the Parliamentary party's hands and did Byron's reputation little good!

summary, suggests that he was officially sent South to report on the condition of affairs in that troubled region. He served as a volunteer and was given a commission as colonel of horse. His report to the Speaker begins: 'Since I departed at Wrexham from my Major-General Sir Thomas Myddelton, being foreclosed towards Wem by Lord Byron's forces, and towards Nantwich by the Irish, and having knowledge both passages to be laid for me; it pleased God, I repaired about ten days before Christmas, through some difficulties, to the good town of Pembroke, which I found environed almost on every side with adverse garrisons.'*

Colonel Thelwall in due course returned to Denbighshire where he played an important part, more prominent, it would seem, as an administrator than as a soldier.

Byron attacked the Cheshire Parliamentarians near Middlewich and defeated them, killing some two hundred. Colonel Robert Byron claimed 300 were slain and 274 taken prisoner. After Beeston Castle was surprised by Captain Sandford, the Royalists, encouraged by this and other successes, laid siege to Nantwich.

The King's party felt the game was now in their hands!

*Quoted in full by Phillips, vol. 2., pp. 140-148.

COLONEL WILLIAM SALESBURY

*This portrait of the governor of Denbigh is from a painting
in the possession of the Right Hon. Lord Bagot at Blithfield. The ship probably records Salesbury's voyage to the
East Indies when a young man*

SERGEANT-MAJOR-GENERAL SIR THOMAS MYDDELTON
The Member for the shire of Denbigh, and the Parliament's commander-in-chief for the six North Wales counties

CHAPTER FIVE

1644

With the arrival of the troops from Ireland the whole complexion of the fighting changed. More were to follow—two infantry regiments under Colonel Robert Byron (a brother to Lord Byron) and Colonel Henry Warren, with four troops of cavalry commanded by Sir William Vaughan who played a prominent part in North Wales for the remainder of the first war. Then came two more infantry regiments under Colonel Robert Broughton of Marchwiel and Colonel Tillier (or Tyllyer). In February Lord Byron ordered the deputy lieutenants of Flintshire to provide mounts for a regiment who had lost their chargers in passage.

Royalists received a reverse on January 12 when Colonel Mytton surprised a party from Chester at Ellesmere, capturing the Chester governor, Sir Nicholas Byron, uncle of Lord Byron, who quickly succeeded him.

Reinforced by the Irish regiments Byron felt confident of capturing Nantwich. It was stubbornly defended by Colonel George Booth. Lieutenant-Colonel Boughton and Captain Thomas Sandford were killed while assaulting the mud walls. Then Sir William Brereton and Sir Thomas Fairfax came to the relief of Nantwich, defeating Byron, and capturing numerous officers of distinction, not the least of whom was George Monck.

Prince Rupert having been appointed President of Wales on February 5, rode to Shrewsbury which he reached on the 18. On March 11 he visited Chester where he was received with ceremony and ardour. Having inspected the outworks and given instructions for their improvement he returned to Shrewsbury taking the Irish veterans with him.

'He visited many of the garrisons in North Wales,' writes Roland Phillips.[54] It would be interesting to know whether the prince journeyed as far as Conway. The arch-

---

[54]*Phillips.* vol. 1. p. 217.

bishop mentions that Rupert 'when he was last in these parts' took men from the local regiment.[55]

Meanwhile on the Shropshire border Mytton was exercising that initiative which was to bring him fame. In June, while watching for a convoy of ammunition sent from Oswestry to Rupert, he learned that a party of musketeers were marching to Bangor-on-Dee. He surprised them at Duddleston and captured 27 out of 54. Only four bore English names. The remaining captives, headed by Quartermaster Owen Jones and Sergeant Richard Foulkes, were all Welsh.

Acting under the Earl of Denbigh, Colonel Mytton attacked Oswestry which was captured on June 24. Welsh soldiers were in the garrison. 'It is a sad sight,' runs a Parliamentary report, 'to behold the ignorance of these Welsh in these parts, and how they are enslaved to serve.'[56]

The list of officers taken includes Captain John Madryn, Lieutenant Nicholas Hookes (surely of Conway!), Cornet Lloyd, Ensign Morgan, Ensign Wynne and Commissary Richard Edwards.[57] Mytton was appointed governor of Oswestry. The Earl of Denbigh learnt that Colonel Marrow meant to attack the town—news which caused him concern for (he wrote):

'my regiment of foot and Sir Thomas Myddelton's are grown so weake that they are not able to guarde their colours.'

His lordship's fears were justified. Colonel John Marrow (who since his return from Ireland, had proved an energetic supporter of the king) led 1,500 horse and 3,500 foot against Oswestry. To frustrate this design Myddelton advanced by way of Whitchurch. He succeeded in putting the Royalists to flight but lost 'one Captain Williams.' Prisoners taken at Oswestry on July 3 included 'twenty Welsh and Shropshire gentlemen.'[58]

---

[55]Ibid. vol. 2. p. 289.
[56]Ibid. vol. 2. pp. 175-6.
[57]Ibid. vol. 2. p. 175.
[58]Ibid. vol. 2. p. 180.

The victors then marched towards Shrewsbury where a skirmish occurred. Here they 'took Major Manley, major to the Lord Byron, and Governor of Bangor, within little more than pistoll shott of their workes.' [59]

This activity accounts for the absence of the Earl of Denbigh and Myddelton from Marston Moor which was fought on July 2. The Marston Moor reverse had a depressing effect on Chester and North Wales which was not lessened by the news that Rupert was riding to Chester, pursued by Brereton and Sir John Meldrum. The defeat had not improved Rupert's temper and he arrogantly demanded more men and money. While Brereton and Meldrum followed the prince, the Earl of Denbigh and Myddelton lay in wait for him, but his Highness outwitted them and reached Shrewsbury on July 20. By August he was again in Chester, quartering his forces over a wide area—some in Chester, some in Shrewsbury, others in Denbighshire and Montgomeryshire.

While in Chester Rupert made fresh demands on North Wales. On August 1 he wrote Lord Bulkeley at Baron Hill requesting him to pay by way of loan to the Archbishop of York the sum of £100 'for my use and his Majesties service.' This was followed on August 8 by a further demand, this time for the loan of 'two peeces of Brasse cannon' to be sent to Chester where the prince was devising improved defences. He obviously was acquainted with the ordnance at Beaumaris for he specifically named the guns as a culverin (18 lb.) and a saker (6 lb.)[60]

On August 5 a party of 550 of Rupert's own horse were surprised at Welshpool by Myddelton and Mytton who captured 40 troopers and 400 chargers while 'Prince Rupert's own cornet was slain.' Sir Thomas Dallison, the officer in charge, 'fled away without his breeches,' in which was found a letter addressed to the prince.[61] Myddelton augmented this useful work by driving off 200 head of cattle from the park of Powys Castle.

While Rupert was at Ruthin, Colonel Marrow led a

[59]Ibid. p. 183.
[60]U.C.N.W. *Baron Hill MSS.* 5372-3.
[61]*Phillips.* vol. 2. p. 194.

party of horse from Chester to Tarvin. On August 21 they were badly defeated by Brereton and Myddelton, Marrow receiving his death wound. The brave officer had married a rich wife but three weeks before. Two regiments of horse rode forth to avenge his death but they, too, were routed. After this second disaster Rupert abandoned his idea of returning to Chester. Accompanied by two hundred horse, including detachments under Colonel Marcus Trevor and Sir William Vaughan,[62] he rode south from Ruthin—no one knew whither. It transpired Bristol was his destination. Vaughan and Trevor must have returned speedily for they were in the fight at Malpas on August 26.

Towards the end of August Myddelton was with Mytton in Oswestry. Orders from London directed Sir Thomas to march into Montgomeryshire, partly to disperse Royalists rallying there; partly to intercept powder which Rupert had sent from Bristol to replenish the diminishing stocks in North Wales and Chester. At this time Sir John Meldrum was endeavouring to recapture Liverpool from the Royalists.

During the night of September 3 Sir Thomas marched his men out of Oswestry and by dawn they were at Newtown where they surprised a small garrison commanded by Sir Thomas Gardiner. In addition to the governor and forty prisoners Myddelton secured thirty-six barrels of gunpowder, twelve barrels of brimstone and a large quantity of match.

His next move was to march on Montgomery Castle where dwelt Lord Herbert of Cherbury. At Myddelton's summons he instantly opened the castle gates and the Parliamentary general was able to store his precious powder inside the walls. Lord Herbert continued to reside in his castle. Myddelton anticipating an attempt by the Royalists to recover the powder, began to replenish the castle with provisions and live stock commandeered from the countryside.

Word of the Royalist loss reached Colonel Robert Broughton who had just been made governor of Shrewsbury, and Sir Michael Ernley. Though in ill health Ernley acted promptly. He summoned aid from all neighbouring

---

[62]*Phillips.* vol. 1. p. 245.

Royalists and, advancing on Montgomery, surprised Myddelton and Mytton during one of their foraging expeditions. Mytton and the infantry took shelter in the castle; Myddelton, who had the worst of the encounter, galloped off with the cavalry to Oswestry.

Then began the siege of Montgomery Castle. The Royalists dug trenches and threw up earthworks, resolved to recapture the powder. Myddelton's determination was to break through the leaguer and rescue Mytton. At the appeal for aid Sir John Meldrum withdrew some of his forces from Liverpool, Brereton marched from Cheshire, while Sir William Fairfax, brother of the future lord-general, added a contingent from Yorkshire, bringing the Parliamentary total to 3,000 men. They converged on Montgomery which they reached on September 17. By this time Ernley's forces were reinforced by those of Sir Michael Woodhouse, now governor of Ludlow, while Lord Byron came with the men of Chester and every available soldier he could recruit in North Wales—2,000 in all.[63]

Leaving a guard for the trenches, Byron (who assumed command) assembled the main body on rising ground behind the town, vacating the site previously occupied by the attackers. This was taken over by the newly arrived Parliamentarians. Both sides remained in these positions until the following day. While a third of the Parliamentary horse were absent in search of provisions Byron made a surprise attack. He beat back Sir John Meldrum's horse and even when the infantry fell to push of pike the Royalists appeared to be gaining the mastery. Sir William Fairfax was captured but was rescued. He then received a wound from which he died next day. Thanks to the Cheshire foot 'who carried themselves more like lions than men,' the Roundheads rallied and completely routed the Royalists, capturing 1,500 men. The prisoners included Colonel Robert Broughton of Marchwiel, Captain Dolben, Captain Morgan, Lieutenant Morgan, Lieutenant Griffiths, and numerous others with Welsh names.

---

[63] *Parry.* p. 386.

Some 500 Royalists were killed. Brereton placed his loss at 40 slain and not 60 wounded. Arthur Trevor, writing to the Marquis of Ormonde, complained:

> 'Our men ran shamefully when they had no cause for so great fear, so that we here are ordained to be the mocking-stock of the War.'

The writer criticizes Lord Byron.

> 'My Lord Byron is infinitely unfortunate, and hath now finished with your Excellency, that is to say, made an end of all your Lordship's army to a man, without any the least service; and truly, my Lord, people now begin to speak out, and say those forces were trifled away by my Lord Byron, who is here observed never to have prospered since his practice to supplant Capel, who is as prudent and valiant a person as the nation affords.[64]

Though one might question his judgment, Archbishop Williams considered the defeat at Montgomery to be worse than Marston Moor.

Myddelton followed up this success by taking Powys Castle on October 2, and with it Lord Powys, his brother, two sons, and 80 officers and men. A parliamentary report ran:

> 'Sir Thomas Myddelton hath now the command of all North Wales, and can raise men there at his pleasure.[65]

In addition to his Chirk estate Sir Thomas Myddelton had a proprietory interest in Ruthin Castle, and, pleased with his recent successes, he resolved to assault it in October 1644. Colonel Marcus Trevor had been appointed governor of Ruthin with a deputy bearing the appropriate name of Captain Sword. Myddelton, according to a letter written by Archbishop Williams, attacked Ruthin on the 19, 'admitted into the town by Trevor and his horse, who ran away, but Sword putting himself into the castle with some 80 men (the place being but in repairing), did beat him away with

---

[64]*Phillips.* vol. 2. p. 209.
[65]*Phillips.* Vol. 2. p. 213.

stones and shot, that upon two of the clock upon Monday he retired to Wem and left 100 men slain behind him.' [66]

If that figure is correct there must have been fierce fighting in the streets of Ruthin.[67]

Peter Roberts in his diary records: 'That upon Sundaee ye xxth Octr. in the ye afternoone, ye enemies, i.e. S'r Thomas Middleton Knt., & his armie, tooke Ruthyn, and imprisoned such male persons as they tooke holde of; & greate rayne and foule weather happened . . . The rebells retorned and fled backe upon Mondaie, God be thanked.'

It is of interest to have Sir Thomas's own account of the incident. He wrote from Red Castle on October 29.

'Having received intelligence of the enemy's fortifying the town and castle of Ruthin, and of the raising of great forces in cos. Denbigh and Flint, being within my limits, by virtue of sending commissions granted to Col. Francis Trafford, a professed Papist, Col. Mark Trevor, Col. Washington, and others, I thereupon, with the few forces I could spare out of my several garrisons of Montgomery and Red Castle, and Col. Mitton's forces from Oswestry, marched to Ruthin, where we found the streets strongly barricaded, the town pretty well fortified, the enemy within it, and Cols. Trevor and Trafford with 120 horse and 200 foot endeavouring to defend the town & oppose us. My foot entering the town broke down the barricades and so made way for the horse, who pursued the enemy's horse through the town and almost to Denbigh, another of the enemy's garrisons, returning in safety with 24 prisoners, including a doctor, cornet and quartermaster. The enemy's foot fled into the castle which I was obliged to leave, Mitton's forces having been recalled to Oswestry upon some pretended fear of the enemy's approach thither, but before quitting the town I caused the turnpikes and fortifications to be broken down and rendered unserviceable. The castle I found to be by nature strong, of large circumference, and situated on a rock, but as

[66]Ibid. p. 2125.
[67]It may have been with the idea of relieving the pressure on Ruthin that Sir John Owen was ordered to rendezvous at Ruabon on October 23.

yet uncovered and the walls under repair. The town adjoining was very considerable, and well suited for a garrison, it being the best situate and fairest and largest town for buildings within that county, and not above 5 miles distant from the enemy's other garrison at Denbigh. If the enemy should settle a garrison at Ruthin and fortify it, they would then be able to curb all the Parliament's friends and their proceedings in cos. Denbigh, Flint, Carnarvon and Anglesey; but on the contrary if you were pleased to enable me to locate a garrison there and fortify the town and castle, I conceive it would be a ready way for the recovery of Denbigh Castle and a speedy reduction of the aforesaid counties.' [68]

The Committee of Both Kingdoms ordered Brereton to send Sir Thomas 500 men 'about Ruthin' which, they suggested, would strengthen Chester's leaguer on that side in Wales. Brereton replied that he would give Myddelton all possible assistance but he could not see how Chester, fifteen miles distant, would benefit.[69]

The appearance of rough troopers in the aristocratic Vale of Clwyd must have come as a rude shock to many residents, particularly those who fondly hoped for better treatment from members of the same cause. Matters grew so serious that on December 12, 1644, the inhabitants and freeholders submitted a petition to Lord Byron when he was staying at Plas-y-ward, the Thelwalls' home near Ruthin. They complained that Trevor's regiment of horse demanded contributions at will, and the petitioners asked that these men should be disciplined as they executed martial law without the consent of the local Commissioners of Array. It was feared that their depredations would ruin the Ruthin market. There had been robberies on the road and they begged that the malefactors should be executed or punished. They asked that the troopers should be distributed evenly all over the lordship, that the inhabitants should be relieved from the 'quartering' of troops and all contributions beyond

[68]Cal. S.P.D. 1644. pp. 80-81.
[69]Ibid. pp. 114 and 133.

the monthly assessment, and that civilians should not be interfered with without the commissioners' authority.[70] Byron admitted the demands were reasonable, coming as they did from loyalists who were willing to adventure their lives and fortunes in the king's service.[71] Colonel Trevor was ordered to make the requisite rearrangements.

Myddelton next captured the fortified abbey of Cwm Hir in Radnorshire. He was joined by Lieutenant-Colonel John Carter who for the rest of his life was to be connected with North Wales. Lieutenant-Colonel Carter accompanied Colonel Beale who was dispatched by the Parliament by sea to assist Myddelton in North Wales. The original intention was for the troops to land in Anglesey but adverse winds drove them into Milford Haven. Here they were able to assist the Parliamentary cause. They marched by way of Cardigan to unite with Myddelton.[72]

Cwm Hir, lying far from the haunts of men, might have been considered immune from attack had not Sir Thomas turned his attention to it. A letter, written from Red Castle on December 9, gives an account of the assault.

'Our General, Sir Thomas Myddelton, having intelligence that the enemy had made them a garrison at Abbey Cwm-Hir, a very strong house, and built with stone of a great thickness, and the walls and outworks all very strong, the house having been in former times an Abbey of the Papists, which is situated upon the borders of Montgomeryshire, within twelve miles of Montgomery, or thereabouts; and the country, by reason of the cruelties, plunder, and unchristian usage of the cruel and merciless enemy towards them, as far as Kery, Newtown, and other places some miles distant, suffered exceedingly, and were almost utterly undone; which, notwithstanding the great strength of the enemy, our General being troubled to hear of the cruelties against the poor people by the enemy, put on a brave resolution, trusting in the Lord, and went

<hr>

[70]*C.W.P.* 1744.
[71]Denb. H.S. Tr. Vol. 3, p. 62.
[72]*Phillips.* vol. 2. p. 219n.

against them and marched thither . . . Our general, being resolved to do his utmost for the gaining of it, summoned the Castle, but the Governor, returned a flat denial and said that he would not deliver up the said garrison to us; whereupon we immediately stormed it, and that with such violence that we soon took it by force . . . . '

'Since which our General having thrown down the enemy's works, and made the garrison unserviceable for the future, we made entrance and marched away from thence to Flintshire, where our General took great care for the securing of those parts and placed a garrison there.'

Sir Thomas Myddelton is said to have asserted he would eat his Christmas dinner in his own home at Chirk. Four days before the twenty-fifth he made an appearance.

'He would not abuse the castle with ordnance (because it was his own house) but fell on with fire-locks at a sink-hole where the governor Col. Watts, was ready to receive him; and gave a pretty number admittance (having an inner work within that hole), but when he saw his opportunity, he knocked them all down that came in, and with muskets killed of the rebels 67, wounded many more, and beat off Sir Thomas, who became so enraged that he plundered his own tenants.'

Colonel Watts gave a more balanced report to Prince Rupert, writing on Christmas Day.

'They lately besieged me for three days; their engineers attempted to work into the castle with iron crows and pickers, under great planks and tables which they had erected against the castle-side for their shelter, but my stones beat them off. They acknowledged in Oswestry they had 31 slain by the castle and 43 others hurt; their prime engineer was slain by the castle-side; they are very sad for him.' [73]

Despite this disappointing reverse Myddelton had every reason to feel satisfied with his year's work and with the condition of Parliamentary affairs in North Wales.

---

[73] *Phillips.* vol. 2. p. 224.

CHAPTER SIX

1645

THE Royalists had lost the initiative. Jubilation followed the landing of the English-Irish army in November 1643 but when the last remnant of these veteran warriors was frittered away by Byron at the Montgomery battle, the pendulum swung. The offensive was now with the Parliamentarians and at the turn of the year Brereton established his advanced headquarters in the village of Christleton, barely a couple of miles from Chester's outworks. The destiny of Chester was linked to the two neighbouring castles (which were in Royalist hands), Beeston on its rocky crag, and Hawarden, five miles along the coastal road into North Wales—the road by which welcome provisions and coal found their way.

It is difficult to determine whether the siege of Chester should be regarded as one long investment or a series of attacks. The Parliamentary menace intensified from January 1645. On January 18 Lord Byron resolved to attack Christleton—which was protected by a mud rampart—burn the place, and, if successful, attempt to relieve Beeston Castle. But the affair was ill-managed, the pace was slow, 'a march rather for May show than a warlike expedition',[74] and Brereton, warned in advance, routed Byron's force, slaying many and taking two hundred prisoners among whom were two colonels and two lieutenant-colonels. Men from Sir Thomas Myddelton's horse and Sir William Myddelton's horse fought under Brereton. The victor wrote to the Committee of both Kingdoms:

> 'Beeston Castle is every day more and more distressed so, unless speedily relieved, I hope a good account may be given therof. If the force we are expecting come to our aid to make good the Welsh side, I hope to give a good account of Chester and all these parts.'[75]

---

[74]*Chester.* XXV. p. 71.
[75]Ibid. p. 70.

About the end of January Brereton and Myddelton 'came over the Dee to Wrexham.'[76] It was evidently their presence there that caused Sir John Owen to march on that important town which changed hands many times during the war.

William Maurice records February 5 as the date on which Prince Maurice reached Shrewsbury. After staying nine days the prince moved towards Chester.

'The first night he lay at Chirk Castle, from thence to Ruthin where S[r] John Owen[s], with the forces of North Wales expected his coming.'

Shortly after this the Parliamentarians, taking advantage of a low tide, forded the Dee estuary and some 2,000 of them appeared before Hawarden Castle now commanded by Rupert's Scout-Master-General, Sir William Neale.

North Wales Royalists did not remain idle in the face of this new threat. On January 29, 1645, the Commissioners of Array ordered that the 'three colonels within the county' of Caernarvon should issue warrants to their several captains to have their companies ready to march with a thousand men to Conway, 'and from thence to the confines of Denbighshire, there to attend the motions of the rebels.'[77]

The situation was so grave that both princes—Rupert and Maurice—marched to raise the siege of Beeston and relieve the pressure on Chester. Events in England were too serious to permit the royal generals to remain long in the vicinity but their approach interfered sorely with Brereton's plans. He fought against time, and on January 26 made an attempt to storm the Chester out-works by night but the glow of matches indicated that the defenders were alert; he had been betrayed. The governor of the city, Lord Byron, meanwhile, appealed to Sir John Owen, who had recently arrived as governor of Conway, to use his influence to secure Welsh forces to march to the relief of the city. Byron complained that he had written volumes of letters and received

[76]*Parry.* p. 351.
[77]*C.W.P.* 1749.

only promises in return,[78] but no performances to help to relieve Chester. Owen soon showed that even if he could not relieve Chester he could provide something more tangible than promises. It was not long before he marched a force to Wrexham (where Brereton had been stationed), hoping to hold the bridgehead at Holt which the Royalists had secured. The news that Rupert had dispatched Maurice to redress the situation caused Brereton to send a strong party of horse and foot under Lieutenant-Colonel Chidley Coote to march through the adjoining parts of Wales to scatter enemy forces. In this they were unsuccessful but brought back 'good store of cattle out of the enemy's quarters including sixty or eighty fit for slaughter which,' observes Brereton, 'will be very serviceable to our garrisons.' The writer informed the Committee that he heard Prince Maurice was at Worcester, intending to march to the relief of Chester—which much encouraged the enemy.[79]

Brereton posted a garrison at Farndon to watch the Royalist garrison at Holt Castle just across the Dee, and he endeavoured to make the best advantage of the time by marching his troops up and down the counties of Flint and Denbigh 'in order to scatter the forces collected therein and intended to join with the prince's army.'

'These are three or four thousand in number,' explains Brereton alluding to the North Wales forces, 'but the greater part being unarmed they fled on our advance first to Ruthin and then to Denbigh.' [80]

The strenuous efforts of the Roundheads proved unavailing and Maurice, on February 19, raised the siege of Chester but he did not feel himself strong enough to attempt the relief of Beeston. The prince, however, ordered a Denbighshire officer, Lieutenant-Colonel John Robinson of Gwersyllt, who at that time was governor of Holt Castle, to attempt to save Beeston. Robinson was unable to break through and, lost a 'Colonel Owen' in the attempt. The prince remained at Chester reducing the perimeter of the outworks

---

[78]*Chester.* vol. XXV. p. 72.
[79]Ibid. p. 73.
[80]Ibid. p. 74.

but allowing his men freedom to roam and plunder. Maurice ordered a solemn fast to be observed and also, on March 4, required all inhabitants to make a 'protestation' of allegiance to the king.

The problem of feeding the several thousand men in the trenches and villages encircling Chester must have been as serious as that of providing victuals for the besieged. From this time the counties of Flint and Denbigh were subjected to a series of raids, ostensibly for sheep and cattle wherewith to feed the hungry troops but records show that burning, slaughter and pillage sometimes marked the trail of the raiders. This lawlessness was not confined to one party. After the forces of Rupert and Maurice had advanced to the relief of Beeston Castle, there were complaints of their ravages. An unknown Parliamentarian in Nantwich on March 25, wrote:

'Since the King's great army lay in these parts the country hath suffered much, and they have been as barbarous in their retreat; for they have not only plundered about Flintshire, Denbighshire, and the borders of Shropshire and Cheshire, but have committed so many murders and rapines, both in these parts, as also in Herefordshire, Worcestershire, and the rest of those places they have been, that the like hath not been heard of. In Cheshire they have not only plundered about Churton, Barton, and Crew, but burnt Farndon, where we kept the pass at Holt Bridge. The Irish and Papists have been at Broughton, and carried away divers Protestants of the town prisoners, and burnt down all the houses in that town. From thence they went to Christleton, and burnt down all that town, the minister's house and the church also.' [81]

Maurice, prior to this, spent one night at Chirk, followed by several at Ruthin where, writes Professor A. H. Dodd, 'a special brew of beer was prepared for him at the borough's expense.' [82] The encouragement afforded the king's party by

[81]*Phillips.* vol. 2. p. 240.
[82]Denb. H.S. *Tr.* Vol. 3. p. 64.

the presence of Prince Maurice was lessened by the disquieting news that royalist Shrewsbury had been surprised on the night of February 22 by Colonel Mytton and Lieutenant-Colonel Reinking, who captured both castle and town without difficulty.

The Shropshire Royalists had troubles enough about this time for on February 15, Colonel John Carter, Captain 'Veiner' (Viner?) and other Parliamentarians surprised and captured Sir Francis Ottley, high sheriff of Shropshire, and with him Mr. Richard Fowler, The Grange, Littleton, with fifteen others at Hinton near Pontsbury.[83]

While Maurice was at Ruthin he issued a commission to Sir John Owen as major-general of foot and directed him to drive all Parliamentarians out of North Wales. With his headquarters at Wrexham (which had been abandoned by Brereton on the advance of the prince) Owen kept part of his force near Holt, some five miles away, to watch the passage of Holt Bridge. The situation had become tense since Colonel Michael Jones, a veteran of the Irish wars, joined the Parliamentarian army in Cheshire where he quickly made a name for himself as a brilliant cavalry commander. Early in March he captured Holt bridge but Sir John Owen counter-attacked and regained possession. Archbishop Williams was enabled to rejoice that the 'Welsh of the mountains' (evidently from his native county of Caernarvonshire) had triumphed. The Royalists' dilemma was sufficiently grave to induce Prince Rupert himself to visit the scene. On March 19 he advanced, pausing at Holt to hang twenty-four countrymen.[84] For some reason Rupert never reached Chester.

Events in England caused the royal generals to hurry away taking with them men badly needed by Byron for the defence of Chester. Their presence, though spectacular, does not appear to have achieved any practical result.

It was on March 13 that Maurice rode out of Chester; by the end of a week the tenacious Brereton had again invested the city. Hawarden, too, was to see the unwelcome

[83] *Parry.* p. 351.
[84] Dodd. Denb. H.S. *Tr.* vol 3. p. 65.

sight of Roundhead headpieces for on April 3 Brereton learnt a convoy of ammunition from Anglesey was on its way to Chester. 'I marched into Flintshire to meet them,' he reported, 'but they, hearing of us, got into Hawarden Castle, whither the country people drove in many carriages, and the malignants fled thither with their wives and children.' Engineers set about undermining Hawarden Castle hoping to secure the good store of powder and ammunition in it. Brereton, on April 3, led the remainder of his force towards Mold until he came to the Davies' ancestral home at Gwysaney 'and fell upon the enemy there, which garrison I took from them, and therein all the Governor (a Captain) and 27 prisoners more, amongst which were some officers.' It seems unlikely that Lieutenant-Colonel Thomas Davies was there, or Brereton would have mentioned the fact. Returning towards Chester by a speedy march 'we gained Manly House from them, killed divers, took a captain and many other prisoners, and wounded many more besides.' [85]

Prince Rupert was expected to come to the aid of Chester again, and the Commissioners of Array for the North Wales counties were ordered to have troops ready to move at an hour's notice to assist the prince. Sir John Owen was particularly active. In addition to defending North Wales he was ordered on April 24 to march to Hereford with 1,000 men.

Meanwhile there was internal friction in Conway. The Archbishop of York complained to Lord Digby: 'Sir John Owen is likewise governor of this place and intimateth a desire to have the Government of this Castle wch his Myte . . . hadd upon high and deare considerations passed over unto me and my assignes, and wch from bare walles I have repayred, victuayled, and ammunicioned at myne owne charges.' He would, he asserted, give a better account of the castle than 'this gentleman' who without this help would never have been able to repair the town. Nor would Owen have had arms to defend it. [86]

At the moment Sir John Owen had enough military

[85] Chester. vol. XXV. p. 80.
[86] Phillips. vol. 2. p. 243.

*1, Colonel Thomas Madryn. 2, Major-General Sir John Owen. 3, Major
David Pennant. 4, Colonel Hugh Wynne*

William Robinson of Gwersyllt, a Commissioner of Array

Colonel John Robinson, one-time governor of Holt Castle

matters to occupy his entire time but not many weeks passed before he was in a position to strike. If a feud was on the point of breaking out in Conway a similar situation was developing in Chester where young Colonel Roger Mostyn had disagreed with the arrogant governor.

Lord Byron, after telling Lord Digby that Prince Rupert had marched off with the remainder of the old Irish regiments, continued:

> '... soe that I was left in the towne with only a garryson of citizens and my owne and Colonell Mostin's regiment, wch both together made not above 600 men, whereof one halfe being Mostin's men, I was forced soone after to send out of towne, findinge them by reason of their officers, who weare ignorant Welch gentlemen, and unwillinge to undergoe any strickt duty, far more precudiciall to us than usefull.' [87]

The Royalists at this particular moment could ill afford to fall out among themselves. On April 15, two of Lord Byron's brothers (there were seven in all serving the king), Sir Richard Byron and Sir Robert Byron, were taken prisoners. While Brereton was intensifying his attacks on Chester and Hawarden, Colonel Michael Jones led a daring raid into the heart of Denbighshire. For this he was accused of allowing his soldiers to indulge in unrestrained pillage. This was only one of several incursions but it is indicative of what was transpiring. Colonel Jones wrote that on April 23 'a party of 500 horse and 400 foot marched into S. Asaph twenty miles distant from Chester where they heard the enemy was. But finding it impossible by reason of their mountaines and castells to overtake them being fled thence, ye County was driven by ye assent of Sr. Th. Middleton for ye gaineing of provisions for ye Army which in a manner until that tyme was provided for by Cheshire, most of which cattel, the whole number of good Cowes not amounting to 400 nor ye sheepe to 2,000 being not fitt to be slaine.'

There follows a reference to a well-known squire's

---

[87]Ibid. p. 246.

house, Plas Ucha, home of an ancestor of Thomas Pennant, the Georgian antiquarian.

'In our returne whence parte of ye Armey passing before Hugh Pennant's house divers of them were shott and one killed, a party being on their march towarde it they forsooke it. To deter others from doing ye like with ye consent of Sr. Th. Middleton ye house was ffired.' Major Hugh Pennant took a prominent part in the 1648 revolt in Anglesey.

Colonel Jones adds: 'Also at ye widdow Hanmer's howse there was a garrison of ye enemyes which killed divers of our men and hindered provisions to be brought unto Hawarden. The howse being summoned and they refuseing quarter it was stormed and all but two put to the sord and ye howse ffired.' [88]

During one of these raids Rhual, the Flintshire home of Baron Evan Edwards, was plundered. Evan Edwards was one of the Commissioners of Array for the county of Flint and had for years been Baron or Clerk of the Exchequer for the County Palatine of Chester. He had built a comfortable home on the outskirts of Mold. His younger brother, Alderman William Edwards, ironmonger, was the leader of the Parliamentary party in Chester, a friend of Sir William Brereton, and later, as a colonel, was put in charge of the captured city.

This family connection was insufficient to protect Rhual.

Baron Edwards had occasion to complain that his house had been stripped and plundered by Captain Coltham and Captain Viner's men, his wife 'stript out of her cloathes by ye Yorkshire men, a box of jewels taken.' Following an investigation Colonel Michael Jones admitted the taking of the jewels but said that though Edwards valued them at £7,000 they were not worth £500. In any event they were of greater use to the public in the Treasurer's hands.[89]

A list of the missing jewels is preserved in the National Library of Wales.[90]

---

[88]*Chester.* vol. XXV. p. 99.
[89]Cal. S.P.D.
[90]N.L.W. *Rhual MSS.* 115.

A NOTE OF THE JEWELLS MY WIFE LOST

Two or 3 seu'all parcells of wyer worke borders some
wth pearle and some Enameld only.

One Border wth Diamonds Rubies & pearle.

One Aggate Chaine thrid wh pearle.

Diverse buttons some inameld wh pearle some wthout
pearle.

Diverse buttons wh Rubies & pearle.

24 gould buttons wh every one a diamond.

21 great wyre worke gould buttons wh pearle whereof
10 of them have Diamonds, 11 Rubies.

1 Chayne of wyer worke wh pearle, one peece of ye
worke like SS.

1 gould bracelett wch goeth 6 or 7 tymes about ones
Arme.

1 great Chayne of Massy gold wh 4 Rubies Inameld 22
diamonds.

1 great gold neckelace wth pearle.

Divers other litle Jewells some sett wh stones some wh
Aggatte.

1 Chayne wh two or three thrids of pearle & a Cornel-
ian betwixt.

1 greate Aggate Chayne thrid wh pearle.

some wyre worke buttons wh one Ruby a peece in it.

28 pommander buttons covered wh gould inameld open
worke, in evry one of the buttons in the Midle a
diamond.

1 One gould Chayne of open worke fild wh pommander
16 diamonds, diverse Rubies and pearle.

Great Company of broad flatt buttons of gould inameld
wth greene white & Red, wh Rubyes.

'I will omitt to mencon what gould silver, Lynen &
Apparell and household stuffe I lost for I am hopelesse
of them but of these, Christyan Charity will move restitution to the Innocent.'

Evan Edwards, who was fined £157 for his delinquency
by the Commissioners for Compounding, has been regarded
as 'a staunch royalist' but the degree of his loyalty is de-
batable. When Major-General Thomas Mytton began his
invasion of North Wales he was evidently accorded so con-

siderate a reception by the 'Baron' that he subsequently issued the following certificate.

'Right ho^{ble}.

I do hereby testifie that Mr. Evan Edwards in November 1645 did voluntarily submitt himself to mee upon my advaunce into Wales before any Garrison was reduced or the Kinge's forces in these p^{ts} subdued. And that he declared his willingness and readynes to serve the parl^t whereupon I graunted him my pass and p'tection. And since, I have had good testimoney of his moderate and fair carriadge when the King's p'tie ruled in the Countrey, and that he was not active against the parliam^t but p'tected the well affected (so farr as lay in his power) from the force and violence of ye king's garrisons. And since that tyme he hath constantly paid contribucon and all other taxacoñs thereunto. All w'ch I humbly submitt to yor hono^{rs} consideracoñ.

Yo^r faithfull & most humble servant,

THO: MITTON.

Halston, primo
decembr, 1646.

'This is a true Copie of Gen'all Mittons Certificate.

WILL EDWARDES.

A similar testimonial (damaged) is in the hand of Lieut.-Colonel G. Gerrard, a veteran who participated in the siege of Chester.

'To all whom these p'ntes may come—Whereas I, Gilbert Gerrard of Crewwood, in the County of Chester, Esq., being in the month of April 1645 comanded by the honourable Sr William Brereton, Baronet, as Lieften't Col.^{ll} of a Regiment of Foot then under the conduct of Col.^{ll} James Louthian to march into the County of Flint to b'seige the Castle of Hawarden in which seidge (torn) Col.^{ll} Louthian comanded in chief (torn) of it for the space of seaven weekes (torn) that I, the said Leif^t Colonell being constant at the Leaguer and taking p'ticular notice of the willingness and readiness of the gent and inhabitants of the said County to contribute to the maintenance and support of the forces ingaged

in the said Leaguer and inquiring of div's [divers] of the inhabitants of the said County touching the dispocoñ and accoñs of the gentry in those p'tes doe make bould to certify that Evan Edwards of Rhuall in the said County Esq., did several times voluntary and freely send unto the said Leaguer greate quantities of all sorts of provision needfull for the same, and upon inquiry made of his disposition and affeceoñ in & unto the late unhappy troubles of the kingdome; I was certified & informed by div'se well affected p'sons that the said Mr. Edwards neu' [never] used any violence or extremity to the Countrey in forcing contribuson to the Commissions of Array when they were in action there. And that the sd Mr. Edwards did also seu'all times advise the Countrey & places thereabout that they should readily contribute to the Parliamt fforces, by whose advice I (torn) thereabout did the more willing (torn) to the said Leaguer. All of which I (torn) witness my hand the xxth day of ffebr, 1646. G. GERRARD.' [91]
In July 1656 Evan Edwards presented a petition to the Protector for his re-admittance to the office of Clerk to the Court of Exchequer of Chester.[92] On July 17, 1660, an Order was issued by the Lords Commissioners of the Treasury to admit Evan Edwards to his office of 'Comptroller of Chester, Bewmaris and Leaverpoole,' granted him by letters patent dated March 29, 1639.[93]

The 'Yorkshire horse' were evidently a source of anxiety to their officers. Sir Thomas Fairfax had to warn the commander not to let his troopers 'spoyle or plunder ye country which they are much condemned for.' The troopers should be punished for such 'wicked courses.' [94]

A more serious transgression was the plundering of the stately mansion on the Caergwrle-Wrexham road known as Plas Têg which belonged to Sir John Trevor, a loyal supporter of the parliament. A list of articles missing has been preserved: It begins with '20 Bedtickes, whereof 7 received back', and ends with '1 faire Bible, 1 Crossbow,

[91]N.L.W. *Rhual MSS.* 136.
[92]Ibid. 122-3.
[93]Ibid. p. 92-53a.
[94]*Chester.* vol. XXV. p. 90.

1 fowlinggunne. 1 great Iron Racke. Brasse of divers Andirons. Brasse Candlesticks. 3 powndes in money. The Cabinet.' This is followed by a note: 'Since then ye foote tooke 3 sheets and one old horse, besides such provisions as they found in ye house.'[95]

These misdemeanours added to the anxieties of Brereton who pleaded that he had not the power to hold the reins of discipline.

It would seem that the raid headed by Colonel Michael Jones was followed by another, shortly after, led by Brereton himself, for the notary public of St. Asaph, Peter Roberts, in his diary entered under the 24th, 25th and 26th of April, 1645: 'Sr. Wm. Brerton and Sr. Tho. Myddleton Kt., with their army, have plyndered St. Asaph's parish, except Wickwer, and made great spoyles, &c. and defiled the Churches there &c.'[96]

Another entry reads: 'uppon Thursday the XVIth of aprill, the Towne and Castle of Denbighe were besieched by ye Parlt. armey, and ye market was uppon ye Wednesday ffollowing kept att the Elme Tree, in the bottom of the Towne, that is, in or neere the Lady Salusbury's House in the lower ende of Denbighe.'[97]

When, under the Self-Denying Ordinance, Sir Thomas Myddelton had to resign his command, the 'great force' he had vaunted in the House had, according to Colonel Michael Jones, dwindled to 160 foot and 70 horse.[98] Colonel Thomas Mytton—whose wife was a sister of the second Lady Myddelton—succeeded Sir Thomas as major-general in North Wales, assuming command in June. News that the king was marching to the relief of Chester perturbed Brereton who despaired of capturing Hawarden Castle. At a council of war on May 19 it was decided to abandon the siege and the following morning, when the tide would serve, the disappointed Roundheads waded back across the fords of the river.[99]

[95]Ibid. p. 91.
[96]*Parry*. p. 368.
[97]*A.&M.* p. 220.
[98]*Chester*. vol. XXV. p. 99.
[99]Ibid. p. 88.

At this time Colonel Mostyn's force was disbanded, but the young commander had not abandoned the royal cause and before long he raised another regiment in time to return to Chester when need was great.

A strange state of affairs existed at Conway. Sir John Owen commanded the walled town but Archbishop Williams tenaciously clung to the castle which he had restored and put into a defensible state. The prelate suffered from no delusions and he had told a kinsman many weeks before that Sir John 'looked big' on the castle and that it was evident he meant to occupy it. Conway was not spacious enough to contain two proud men and the inevitable blow fell one evening in May.

The manner in which Sir John struck is set forth in a remonstrance which the indignant prelate sent to King Charles shortly afterwards.

> 'Upon the 9th of May, 1645, Sir John Owen, Governor of Conway, about seven of the clock in the evening, before the night guard was sent into the castle, the possession thereof was placed by the King in the Archbishop of York, and his assigns, upon great and valuable considerations by his gracious Letters . . . . did with bars of iron, and armed men, break the Locks and Doors, and enter into the said Castle, and seize upon the Place, the Victuals Powder, Armes and Ammunition, laid in by the said Archbishop at his own charge.'

The prelate demanded that the 'rabble of grooms and beggarly. people' should be prevented from filching the goods stored there, but Sir John 'in a furious manner utterly refused it,' and threatened to seize the plate and other valuables for his own use 'than which no rebel or enemy could deal more outrageously.'

Even Owen's kinsman and namesake, the Bishop of St. Asaph, could not prevail upon him to exercise more consideration.

Out the archbishop had to go, and he withdrew to his own house at Penrhyn, near Bangor.[100]

Sir John justified his conduct by writing to the king accusing Williams of treachery. To this complaint Charles replied:

'You should be very cautious how you proceed to lay Imputations upon him of so high a nature'—and required Owen to pay proper respect to the prelate.

Between the seizing of Conway Castle and the king's reply to Owen's accusation the battle of Naseby had been fought.

The turmoil of the proud prelate's thoughts must be imagined after he had returned to the demesne of his forebears, or as he paced the tree-lined walks of lovely Gwydir when he visited his favourite niece, Grace, who had married Owen Wynn. The time of his greatness when he was Lord Keeper of the Great Seal and the confidant of King James, the spacious days of his palace at Buckden, the throne in the minster at York, must have seemed a distant dream. He was a Caernarvonshire man again, back among his own people, and his people were faced with dire calamity.

Later he wrote: 'What they will say in the end of the day I do not know, nor do I care, if I could with mine own sacrificing keep this poor country from being ruined.' Their well-being might have then appeared of greater consequence than a tottering throne. This was the altruistic aspect. To it must be added his personal reaction—a sense of outraged dignity, and resentment at the broken pledge of the monarch he trusted. Despite this discouragement he continued to exert his influence for the royal cause, and no man laboured more assiduously than the archbishop in endeavouring to bring relief to besieged Chester.

---

[100]The Remonstrance is printed in the appendix to vol. I. *The Heart of Northern Wales*, W. Bezant Lowe, and in R. Williams' *History and Antiquities of the Town of Aberconwy*.

CHAPTER SEVEN

THE extent of North Wales's participation in the memorable battle of Naseby is still undetermined. That some Welsh soldiers were there is apparent for in the county archives in Caernarvon are records of old soldiers who appealed for pensions as some recompense for wounds suffered on that fateful day. These simple entries tell their own tale.

'Robert Owen of Caerhun, maymed of the hand and wounded on the head in Nasebie fight, a very poor man.'
'John Williams of Pethkelert in Nasby fight hurt in the legge and the thighe, a great wound.'

Of the regiments in which they served, of the officers who led them, no word is penned. Nor is there a list of those who fell. Imagination must fill many gaps.

When that decisive conflict left the New Model Army victors on the field the king sought shelter in the marches of Wales. Charles's aimless wanderings for the next few months are those of a bemused man, stupified by calamity yet stubbornly resolved not to yield. He rambled from place to place, seeking entertainment at Raglan, at Ludlow, at Cardiff, talking, among other matters, of making a last stand in the Snowdon mountains. There was even a wild scheme for smuggling the young Duke of York across to Dublin from Beaumaris in Captain Bartlett's *Swan* but nothing came of it. By September Charles finally made up his mind. He would move north through loyal Lancashire and join forces with the victory-winning Marquis of Montrose in Scotland.

Protected by his faithful cavalry the king rode north. The itinerary was faithfully recorded by a gentleman trooper, one Richard Symonds, who rode in the Earl of Lichfield's troop. The officer in charge of his Majesty's life-guard was a Herefordshire soldier, Sir William Vaughan, whose presence in North Wales was soon to be felt. The king, having raised the siege of Hereford, resolved to head for

73

Chester which was then in sore straits. Symonds noticed that their movements were watched by 'the nearest enemy' —Roundhead cavalry commanded by Poyntz and Rossiter who were specially deputed to keep an eye on the royal movements. Attention naturally centres on the New Model Army but it was not the only force under the new Parliamentary administration. There was, in addition, a Northern Army commanded by a veteran professional soldier of the Continental wars, Colonel-General Sydenham Poyntz.

On Thursday, September 18, word reached the royal party that the foe lay between them and Worcester, so Charles rode to Presteign where the night was spent. Over the mountains they went next day to Newtown, barely sighting a house after the first three miles. The next stage carried the cavalcade to Llanfyllin, passing *en route* Gregynog, the home of Sir Arthur Blayney, a devoted Montgomeryshire loyalist who later had his elbow shattered in the Beaumaris fight of 1648. Then, 'over the mountains to Chirk' where the governor, Colonel John Watts, was waiting to receive his Majesty in a home worthy of the occasion. The royal guards lay that night at Llangollen. While he was at Chirk Charles received the unwelcome news that the enemy had carried Chester's outworks. Instantly a messenger was dispatched to Lord Byron bidding him hold out another twenty-four hours as the king was coming to his rescue. Events were now shaping which were to terminate in the battle known as Rowton Moor or Rowton Heath.

On Tuesday, September 23, the king's force left Chirk. With his Majesty rode a number of noblemen, including General Lord Charles Gerard 'with his gallant troop of lifeguards.' Three brigades were commanded by Sir Marmaduke Langdale, Sir Thomas Blackstone, and Sir William Vaughan.

Holt Bridge, which changed hands so frequently, appears at this time to have been in possession of the Parliamentarians, or else destroyed, for the horsemen crossed the Dee by a bridge of boats. Hereabout the force divided. Advancing during the darkness Langdale led three brigades down the Cheshire bank of the river. 'Their business,'

74

Symonds explains, 'was to fall upon those horse and foot which lay before Chester.'

The king continued down the Welsh side of the Dee and crossing by the old bridge, entered the city where he was joyfully welcomed. He slept that night at the house of Sir Francis Gamull in Bridge Street with guards on duty in the road outside.

Meanwhile Poyntz, faithful to the trust imposed upon him, had doggedly followed in the wake of the unsuspecting royal army. He might have caught the Royalists utterly unprepared had not Sir Richard Lloyd, governor of Holt Castle, intercepted a letter. It was written by Poyntz and was directed to Colonel Michael Jones thanking him for standing his ground notwithstanding the king's approach. Poyntz told him of the king's 'tired over-marcht horse', which, he intimated, he meant to attack as soon as he overtook them.

The alarming news was speedily forwarded. It put Sir Marmaduke Langdale on his guard. On the morn of Wednesday, September 24, this veteran cavalryman faced his brigade about on the Chester side of the Dee and marched back to a spot known as Hatton Heath. Here he sighted the advancing Parliamentarians whom he charged so vigorously that he 'beat them back and took some cornets'.

Charles lost the battle of Rowton Moor not through any lack of courage of his troops but from sheer ineptitude on his part. The original plan was for Sir Marmaduke Langdale to assault the Roundheads who besieged Chester. During the engagement the besieged were to issue from the city and attack them in the rear. The opposite transpired. Poyntz's unexpected appearance distracted Langdale, and while he was reassembling his men on Rowton Moor, a mile nearer the city than Hatton Heath, he found himself attacked from behind by Colonel Michael Jones and Adjutant-General Louthian who, with 500 horse and 300 foot rushed from the trenches to aid the northern general.

Their hasty movements created the erroneous impression that they were in flight, and a considerable portion of Chester's garrison sallied out of Northgate to pursue them.

Eastgate had been blocked up. A furious contest had taken place on Rowton Heath, and Langdale's men were routed. Poyntz pursued the fleeing Cavaliers almost to Chester walls where the victors were checked by Lord Gerard and the Earl of Lindsey who had drawn up their troops in the open.

"But those disordered horse which fled with Sir Marmaduke, had crowded all the little passes and narrow lanes between Hoole Heath and the city, a ground quite unfit for horse to fight upon; so that when a fresh body of the enemy's musketeers charged resolutely upon them, they forced the king's horse to turn and route one another, and overbear their own officers who would have restrained them.' [101]

A sorry sight it must have been for Charles, watching from the top of the Phoenix Tower. Earlier in the day the king had climbed to the cathedral tower but a cannon ball carried off the head of an officer beside him and his Majesty descended to a less conspicuous vantage point.

It is estimated that over 600 men lost their lives on Rowton Moor. Among them was Bernard Stuart, the handsome young Earl of Lichfield in whose troop Richard Symonds served. Following the death of his leader Symonds transferred to Vaughan's brigade. Among the prisoners was Lieutenant-Colonel Broughton.

An unusual sidelight on the battle is contained in a memorandum written on a blank page of Clarendon's *History* by Peter Shakerley, son of Colonel Sir Jeffrey Shakerley who commanded a regiment under Sir Marmaduke.

'Poyntz coming in a marching posture along the narrow lane between Hatton Heath and Rowton Heath, Sir Marmaduke, having lined the hedges, fell upon him, and killed a great many of his men; and having so, ordered Colonel Shakerley, who was best acquainted with that country, to get the next way he could to the king (who lodged then at Sir Francis Gamull's house in Chester) and acquaint him that he had obeyed his orders in beating Pointz back, and to know his

[101]*Hemingway.* vol. I. p. 183.

Majesty's further pleasure. The colonel executed his orders with better speed than could be expected; for he galloped directly to the river Dee, under Huntingdon house, got a wooden tub (used for slaughtering of swine) and a batting staff (used for batting coarse linen) for an oar, put a servant into the tub with him, and in this desperate manner swam over the river, his horse swimming by him (for the banks there were very steep, and the river very deep), ordered his servant to stay there with the tub for his return, and was with the king in little more than a quarter of an hour after he left Sir Marmaduke, and acquainted the king, that if his Majesty pleased to command further orders to Sir Marmaduke, he would engage to deliver them in a quarter of an hour, and told the king of the expeditious method he had taken, which saved him going nine or ten miles about, by Holt-bridge (for the boats at Eaton were then made useless); but such delays were used by some about the King, that no orders were sent, nor any sally made out of the city by the king's party till past three o' clock in the afternoon, which was full six hours after Poyntz had been beaten back; and so Poyntz having all that time for his men to recover their fright they had been put into in the morning, Poyntz rallied his forces, and with the help of the parliamentary forces who came out of the suburbs of the city to his assistance (upon whom the King's party in the city might have fallen) put all those of the king's to the route, which was the loss of the king's horse, and of his design to join Montrose in Scotland.' [102]

Richard Symonds evidently fought all through the battle and after entering in his diary an account of Langdale's victory over Poyntz at Hatton Heath, all he could wearily add was 'But they beat us agen for't.'

It was no longer safe for King Charles to remain in the city. He gave orders to Lord Byron and the commissioners 'that if, after ten days, they saw no reasonable prospect of relief, to treat for their own preservation.'

---

[102]Quoted in full by Pennant and Hemingway.

The following morning, September 25, between 9 and 10 o'clock, Charles rode across the Dee Bridge, screens having been erected to conceal the movements of the troops, and at the head of five hundred horsemen, crossed the marsh and found security in Hawarden Castle. Here the fugitive monarch stayed three hours as guest of the governor, Sir William Neale. While the king rode to Denbigh, which he reached that night, Sir Marmaduke Langdale rallied his scattered troopers by appointing a rendezvous two miles from Holt Castle.

When the trampling of five hundred chargers sounded on the night air every citizen of Denbigh must have been tiptoe with excitement. At the foot of Lower Street lay the building of the Carmelite Friary, by that time known as The Abbey. The cavalcade toiled up the long hill, past the old Cross at the approach to High Street, and through the mighty Burgess Gate which gave admittance to the old town, and so to the great gate of the castle where the loyal governor, Colonel William Salesbury of Bachymbyd, *Hên Hosannau Gleision* (Old Blue Stockings) awaited to greet the liege lord he served so well. The governor had received his commission from the king two years before, and the castle had been restored by him and his kindred at their own cost.

'Friday, 26 Sept., rested.' This succinct entry in Symonds' diary speaks volumes.

The weary monarch would have had much to meditate upon—his loyal troopers cut down in the Rowton fight and nine hundred prisoners taken to Nantwich 'whereof about twenty were of the king's own troop.'

Charles lodged in the tower called the Great Kitchen, subsequently to be known as the King's Chamber. Colonel Salesbury 'spoke so plainly to his Majesty for two hours in private, that the good king said, "Never did a prince hear so much truth at once!"' [103] Having done so, Old Blue Stockings made a vow he would never deliver up the castle save on the instructions of the king himself.

[103] A.&M. p. 232.

Lord Digby was with the party and wrote to Sir John Owen at Conway bidding him attend. Archbishop Williams also arrived at Denbigh. 'Here is now with his Majesty, the Archbishop of York, Sir John Owen and divers others', wrote Digby to Lord Byron from Denbigh on September 26.[104] Whether a reconciliation was achieved is not known but two significant facts emerge; one, that Sir John remained governor of Conway; the second is that the prelate continued to labour with undiminished ardour in the royal cause, and even wrote to Owen:—

'Sir John, I pray you be confident that I loue you and Honnour you, and, if you please to believe it, with the best understanding that God hath giuen me, well be readye to runne the same fortunes with you in this dangerous tyme and business.[105]

Symonds writes: *Satturday, 27, was a general rendezvous 3 miles from Denbigh.*

A hamlet known as Cyffylliog was chosen as the place of meeting, presumably favoured for its remoteness and because it lay approximately an equal distance from the castles of Ruthin and Denbigh. Green hills slope down to a vale where runs a sizeable stream in which cavalry men could water their mounts. Walls of water-rounded stones line the narrow roads which converge from several directions, and the little church is guarded by age-old yews. It is hard to conceive Charles, King of England and Scotland, in such a setting. In the church register was a page—subsequently extracted—which contained the following entry:

'Saturday, 27th. September, 1645. Be it remembered, that King Charles was the day and year above written, making his rendezvous in the parish of Cyffylliog, in a place there called Cenfesydd.'

A service was held in Denbigh church on Sunday morning, probably the garrison church at St. Hilary of which only the tower remains. Symonds records:

[104]*Cal. S.P.D.* pp. 160-1.
[105]*Arch. Camb.* 1875.

'About one of the clocke afternoon, the K. marched through Ruthyn, where there is a large castle and fortified, to Chirke Castle, com. Denbigh. Watts knighted. Here P. Maurice met us with his troope, and those of P. Rupert's horse that came from Bristoll, Lucas's horse, &c. toto 600 or 700.'

And so to Bridgnorth, and finally Newark and Newcastle. Wales never saw Charles again. The king ordered Sir William Vaughan to return to North Wales with his brigade to effect the relief of Chester.

With Symonds' meticulously kept diary for reference it is difficult to account for the peculiar story that the king fled to Llanrwst where the bridge was broken down to prevent pursuit!

Naseby is generally accepted as marking Charles's downfall, but after Naseby there was still some slight possibility of a rally in the west. After Rowton Moor no such hope remained. The king's fortune was past recovery.

Standing amid the ruins of Denbigh's mighty walls today, one may imagine the sombre thoughts which passed through the royal mind as the Stuart gazed down on the verdant vale so soon to be scarred by the earthworks of his rebellious subjects.

CHAPTER EIGHT

THE effect of the Self-Denying Ordinance was soon felt by the Parliamentary forces in Cheshire for on June 13, 1645, Sir William Brereton had been recalled to London, not only to answer the charges made against his troops for plundering, but also to serve as Knight of the Shire. The military command he held from the outset was vested in a committee, the only concession being that he was chosen one of the five members. It was not until the middle of October that Sir William was able to return to his duties in the field and in his absence Rowton Moor was fought. Colonel Mostyn evidently made his peace with Lord Byron for, during the disturbance occasioned by the battle, he and Colonel Hugh Wynne of Bodysgallen with all the forces they could muster slipped through the cordon and rejoined the defenders in the beleaguered city.

Both sides were particularly alert, the Royalists to avert further disaster, the Parliamentary party to make the most of their triumph. The king was depressed by the news that Montrose had been defeated (at last) at Philiphaugh.

The tidings had not found their way into the streets of Chester but Byron was filled with foreboding and, three days after Rowton Moor, he wrote to Lord Digby at Denbigh: 'I do not like this return of Poyntz's horse. I fear something is amiss with my Lord of Montrose. All that can be done for the present is that the King raise the whole force of Wales and command the horse immediately to advance this way.' [106] The Parliamentary batteries opened a fierce fire on Chester.

Though the king with his hundreds of horsemen headed for the English border, he had turned his back on Chester merely in a literal sense. The loyal city was much in his mind and heart. The course he adopted is indicated in another letter sent by Lord Digby to Lord Byron in Chester.

'His Majesty is advanced as far as Newark and we hope it will have the wished result of drawing the rebels

---

[106]*Chester.* vol. XXV. p. 124.

great body of horse from the Welsh side of Chester. As for any parties they may leave, his Majesty will instantly send back Sir W. Vaughan with strength enough to master them.' [107]

The letter is dated October 5.

Sir William Vaughan concentrated on collecting forces from the various garrisons along the marches of Wales until by the middle of October he felt himself strong enough to attempt to relieve Chester. In his efforts he was loyally supported by the Royalists of North Wales. Archbishop Williams was at Beaumaris endeavouring to load a vessel with provisions in the hope that it could get through the blockade and reach Chester by water. Sir John Owen was to raise a force of cavalry though on this occasion he does not appear to have exhibited his customary zeal. Colonel Roger Mostyn escaped from Chester, crossed to Dublin, and managed to recruit some more soldiers for the king though the numbers fell below his expectation. The Lord St Pol—Byron's general-of-horse—also managed to get through the Parliamentary lines and reached Rhuddlan where he conferred with Colonel Gilbert Byron, Lord Byron's brother. The archbishop had arranged for the foot-men of Caernarvonshire to rendezvous at Groes-yn-Eirias (Colwyn Bay)[108] there to be joined by a party of horse before they marched to Denbigh. The delay experienced here proved, as it transpired, their salvation.

There was to be a general rendezvous on Denbigh Green which (until enclosed by Act of Parliament in 1807) extended from the Friary fields as far as Trefnant on one side and the forest of Lleweny on the other.[109] Vaughan advanced from Montgomeryshire to unite with the North Wales infantry. His movements were not unknown to Brereton who had recently returned from London and the Cheshire baronet made arrangements accordingly.

Symonds now served under Vaughan and, thanks to his

---

[107]*Cal. S.P.* Dom. (1645). p. 174.
[108]Prof. A. H. Dodd. Denb. H.S. *Tr.* vol. 3. p. 70.
[109]*A.&M.* p. 270.

invaluable diary, it is possible to trace the royal army's progress.

Vaughan's advance guard reached Chirk Castle at 9 a.m. on October 23, the general following more leisurely. Symonds records:

'Munday, October 26. Sir William Vaughan came to Chirke. We marched to Llanannis [Llanynys], Mr. Thelwall's howse, com. Denbigh.'

This unusual diarist had a fondness for heraldry and missed no opportunity of slipping into a parish church to note heraldic adornments on tomb or painted glass. Even on the eve of battle he found time to jot down comments on the churches at Ruthin and Llanrhaeadr. On the last day of October Vaughan was at Denbigh.

Across the border Brereton was active. He dispatched Colonel Michael Jones with 1,500 horse and Adjutant-General Louthian with 1,000 foot to scatter the Royalist muster. On October 30 the Roundheads reached Mold. The next day they marched to Ruthin where Vaughan had paused so short a time before. Here they were joined by 'that active officer' Thomas Mytton, who, as the new major-general assumed command. The Roundheads appear to have taken Vaughan by surprise when, the following morning, they marched down the road from Ruthin. This is the more unaccountable because of an entry in Symonds' diary.

'Friday, October 31. came intelligence to Denbigh to Sir William Vaughan that the enemy under the command of Mitton was advanced to Ruthyn, both horse and foot.'

Denbigh's square-towered parish church of St. Marcella, known as Whitchurch, stands isolated on the common. At the foot of Denbigh's long northern approach was the ruined friary consisting of several buildings with a few trees nearby. Otherwise little broke the wide expanse of Denbigh Green though quicksets bordered the narrow roadways. It

The Battle of Denbigh Green fought between a Parliamentary force under Major General Thos. Mytton and Royalists under Sir William Vaughan. November 1, 1645

was here the entire Royalist force assembled on the morning of November 1. Their total is given as 1,700 horse and 400 infantry. Their musketeers and dragoons lined the hedges which flanked the road from Ruthin—and waited. Those who felt chill on that damp, drab morning would shortly be warmed by exercise.

'Satturday at noone wee had the alarm, for they were at Whitchurch below the towne. Their approach was handsomely disputed by our horse and foot about an howre in the hedges and lane.'

So wrote Symonds. This was the first stage of the battle as seen through a Royalist's eyes. The Parliamentary report ran as follows:

'The Forlorn Hope, forty out of every regiment, was commanded by Capt. Otter, Captain of the Reformadoes,[110] a gallant soldier, and Captain William Edwards,[111] a Cheshire Captain and well-deserving gentleman, who, coming to Whitchurch, a mile from Denbigh, were in a lane flanked by the enemy's horse and dragoons, so that they were forced to make good that pass with the Forlorn Hope and Cheshire dragoons, under the command of Capt. Finch and Capt. Holt, stout and resolute men. These, with the Forlorn Hope, behaved themselves gallantly, and maintained the pass till the foot came up, the most part of which, with the Warwick and Derbyshire horse, Commanded by Major Sanders and Major Hokesworth, seconding the Forlorn Hope, bare the burden of the day, whilst the Reformadoes, Cheshire horse, and 400 Lancashire foot, were intended for a greater service; for the Commanders finding that straight lane too difficult a pass to fall through upon the enemy, were marshalled in open field.' [112]

Symonds takes up the story.

[110]Reformadoes were officers waiting for regiments to be re-formed.
[111]This might be Alderman William Edwards, Brereton's friend, and a younger brother of "Baron" Evan Edwards of Rhual. He was later a colonel.
[112]*Phillips.* vol. 2. pp. 282-3.

'There number of foot, being 1,500 at least, made ours retreat to the towne, which was not long disputed by reason of their forward advancing. Our horse were putt to a disorderly retreat, notwithstanding Sir William Vaughan drew many of them up upon a greene neare two myles off but could not be made to stand; a party of Arcall horse charged the persuers, and were seconded by part of Prince Maurice's life-guard. The foot were let into the castle by the governor. The horse gott to Llanrwst that night, com. Denbigh, twelve miles distant. Next morning dispersed to quarters. The governour of Denbigh wrote that the enemy was in his sight above double our number.'

It was on the advice of 'some who knew the country', that Mytton moved his troops into the open.

'These last mentioned were drawn thence by Denbigh Green, a way near four miles in compass, to fall upon the enemy upon even ground, which, whilst drawn off, the foot (exceeding forward to engage themselves on the whole) beat the enemy out of the lane, and routed both horse and foot, driving them under the command of the castle, where they rallied themselves; but the Forlorn Hope, Derby and Warwick horse, with the foot, encountered them again, and utterly routed them, whom the horse chased eight miles in the way to Conway, making great execution on the way, taking many prisoners, and 500 or 600 horse, and so long pursued that not above seven score were left together . . . It is conjectured by those who are best able to give account herein, that above 100 of the enemy were slain, about 400 taken prisoners, with divers men of quality. It is not known that any of ours are slain, and few wounded.

The dispatch was dated from the town of Denbigh which the victorious troops had occupied. An interesting echo of the flight to Llanrwst is preserved in the *Calendar of Wynn Papers*.

'On Allhallowtide twelvemonth, 1645, Sir William Vaughan, having been defeated near Denbigh by Gen.

86

Mytton, fled with the remainder of his horse, in number 900, towards the mountains, and fell that night upon the house of Sir Richard Wynn, where they stayed five days, and, on going, rifled the house.' [113]

A tumultuous time for tranquil Gwydir!

Williams asserts that the pursuit continued as far as Llangernyw. Cannon-balls supposed to have been fired in a skirmish there have been dug up in the village.[114] It is said that several soldiers killed at the time are buried in the churchyard under the east window.

Though there were several conflicts in North Wales, Denbigh Green is probably the only one meriting the description of battle. William Maurice in his diary records:

'Sir William Vaughan came with two or three thousand men out of Ludlow, and other garrisons in the marches of Wales, marched through Montgomeryshire towards Denbigh Castle, intending with the addition of the forces of North Wales, to relieve Chester agayne; but Colonel Mytton, hearing of his approach, drew up his forces towards him, and neare Denbigh Castle, gave him battel, wherein Sir William Vaughan was overthrown with all his army, whereof many were slayne in the pursuit, which continued six miles, even to Llangernyw.'

From his vantage on the castle ramparts Colonel Salesbury looked down upon the turmoil on the fair plain below. That night, when the tumult was over he penned a line to the discomfited commander.

'For Sir William Vaughan.
'Sir,—I wish you to be as free from danger as I hope we are secure and in good condition here. On your foot being perceived under the castle wall I received them in tho' I conceived I had no need of them for the defence of this place, yet having, I doubt not, provision enough, their valour and good service withall meriting

[113]*C.W.P.* 1810.
[114]*A.&M.* p. 218.

my compassion, I freely entertained them. I judge the enemy had a force that came the other way over the Green, equal in number or thereabouts, to what you fought with. Mitton and the foot I am informed quarter in the town and most of the horse in the country about: God bless us all!

Your friend and servant,

William Salesbury.

Denbigh Castle, 1st Nov. 1646 (*sic*)—7 at night.

What you may resolve to take I leave to your own discretion.' [115]

Colonel Salesbury's ejaculation of surprise betokens his amazement at the Royalists' defeat. The victorious troops do not appear to have remained long in the vicinity of Denbigh. They had achieved their object and their presence was required at the leaguer before Chester.

Symonds records that by November 4 the Royalist foot were able to march from the castle to Llanrwst. A list of regiments comprising Vaughan's army includes 200 horse under Colonel Whitley of Aston.

It speaks well for the tenacity of the Royalists of North Wales that, undiscouraged by the reverse, they immediately devised fresh plans for the relief of Chester.

On November 18 Brereton was able to inform the Speaker that Beeston Castle had surrendered after a siege of twelve months. The gallant governor, Captain Valet, with fifty soldiers was permitted to march to Flint, and from thence to Denbigh and Beaumaris. The dauntless garrison in Chester, made a gallant though unsuccessful attempt to blow up a bridge of boats by which the Roundheads spanned the Dee.

On Christmas Day Colonel John Carter (who was active on the Welsh side) frustrated an attempt by Welsh Royalists to drive a hundred head of cattle to the city. The relief train had almost reached Holywell when the watching Roundheads were detected and the cattle were scattered for safety among the hills.[116]

---

[115]*Newcome* (*Denb.*). pp. 65-66.
[116]*Chester.* vol. XXV. p. 144.

A few days later Carter's patrol was outwitted. A hundred Cavaliers galloped through the cordon and reached the city. Each horseman was burdened with seven stone of meat in addition to some oatmeal and powder. The Parliamentarians only succeeded in snapping up a cornet and a trooper as the daring adventurers broke through. From these prisoners information was extracted. They learned that in the city the poor had revolted and were cursing Lord St Paul as 'a French rogue.' [117]

General Mytton established himself at Wrexham with his force, the town becoming also the headquarters of the Parliamentary county committee for Flintshire.

At low tide on December 30 Brereton's horse crossed from Blacon Point and thrust towards Mold, Northop and Denbigh. The foot were carried across in boats to strengthen the lines on the Welsh bank. The following day Brereton advanced to Whitchurch with 1,500 horse and as many foot[118]—too imposing a body for the valiant Blue Stockings to attack. 'The duty is extremely hard and much provision wanting,' wrote Brereton.

The Parliamentary soldiers' hardships were slight compared with the suffering endured in Chester. Welsh warriors died of starvation. Great stones, hurled over the walls into the devoted city, spread death and destruction. In order to frustrate any attempt to land provisions from Conway, Rhuddlan and Beaumaris, where a woman spy reported preparations were being made, Brereton armed two small vessels. These were under the command of Captain Stephen Rich, the same who, some time before, sailed up the Dee and bombarded Chester with the two small guns with which his ship was equipped.

During the terrible siege of Chester the defenders included such North Wales officers as Colonel Roger Mostyn, Colonel Hugh Wynne, Lieutenant-Colonel John Robinson, Lieutenant-Colonel Peter Griffith and Captain Richard Griffith of Llanfair Isgaer.

A vivid picture of the sufferings of the besieged is con-

---

[117]Ibid. p. 165.
[118]Ibid. p. 157.

tained in a journal kept by one of the garrison. The original is in the British Museum (Harleian MS. 2155) and is printed in detail in The Chester and North Wales Archaeological and Historic Society's *Journal XXV* from which these extracts are taken:

> 'By this time they have unmusled death and sweare theyle let him loose amongst us, a wide mouth'd morterpiece in which like the mouth of Etna spitts litte mountaines in our faces and grinds our dwellings into dust and ashes.

> 'They sent us two Welsh granadoes and beat downe the end of a house in Eastgate Street without doing further harm.

> 'Eleven huge granadoes like so many tumbling demyphaetons threaten to set the city, if not the world on fire. This was a terrible night endeed, our houses like so many splitt vessels crash their supporters and burst themselves in sunder through the very violence of these descending firebrands.

> 'But for all this they are not satisfied, women and children have not blood enough to quench their fury, and therefore about midnight they shoot seven more in the hope of greater execution.

> 'Either there granadoes are all spent, or elles they are too costly, and therefore to kill us with less charge, they toss us three huge stones.

> '*Dec. 25.* Because it is a festivall, instead of stones they send us in a token four granadoes, one of which burst among themselves.'

Amid cold and hunger the old year[119] passed to the thunder of mortar and culverin.

---

[119]Throughout this book the year is taken to start on January 1.

CHAPTER NINE

1646

THIS, the last year of the first Civil War, might well be remembered as 'the year of sieges'. Though it represented twelve months of continuous strife there was little fighting in the open field. The utmost endeavours of both factions centred on Chester.

On January 2 Archbishop Williams, seated in his own house in Conway, penned a letter to the Marquis of Ormonde, replying to a missive which the marquis had sent from Ireland on December 12 and which had, the previous day, come to hand. For a communication to take nearly three weeks to travel from Dublin to Conway suggests adverse winds or a particularly vigilant Parliamentary cruiser. The feud with Sir John Owen had abated sufficiently to permit the prelate to sojourn in Conway. The house, sometimes termed Parlwr Mawr or the Bishop's Palace, stood near Telford's 'Bangor Gate' where sorry fragments of its demolished walls may still be seen. Williams reported that sufficient relief from the Welsh side had reached Chester to enable the garrison to hold out another three weeks. The provisions would have lasted longer had it not been for the demands of homeless people from the suburbs whose houses had gone up in flames. 'The Mayor's wife [Charles Walley was mayor in 1644, and in 1645 there was no civil election] always suspected, is gone over to the enemy. Our forces from Wales, of some 100 horse (for foot we have none), under the conduct of Major Evet, put in this last supply of meal and powder, whilst the enemy were withdrawn in part to meet Sir William Vaughan, lingering at High Ercall [in Shropshire] with 1,500 horse and foot in expectation of the main supply from Oxford and Worcester under the Lord Astley and Sir Charles Lucas, who should add unto his number in horse and foot, 2,200 more. We of the Welsh being quite frightened (and three of our five counties being for a great part of them under contribution to the enemy), are not able to make above 300 horse, and scarce so many foot, being by a piece of illconduct in Prince Rupert when he was last in these parts, quite disarmed and discouraged.' [120]

Relief from Ireland was expected but the archbishop wrote that he dare not advise the marquis to send more troops until it was seen what Vaughan intended to do. While he was writing there was in his house 'a French Lord, who serves the King, Mons. de Saint Pol' who expected Vaughan to advance from Much Wenlock into Wales during the week. It might be possible for the forces from Ireland to land and wait in Anglesey or Caernarvonshire until the cavalry from the border could co-operate. But by the twenty-fifth no transports had dropped anchor in Beaumaris roads and the prelate confided in Lord Digby that there was 'no relying upon these Irish forces.'

By that time a body of North Wales loyalists had mustered for the relief of Chester. They were led by Colonel Gilbert Byron, governor of Rhuddlan Castle, and Lord St Pol (St. Paul) who had 500 horse and foot, to which were added 'a piece of a regiment' (160 men) raised by Colonel Roger Mostyn in Ireland who brought both English soldiers and mercenaries from Lorraine.[121]

But all this came to naught for Mytton pounced before a junction with the English forces could be affected. He chased the fleeing Royalists through Denbigh and Ruthin. Chester abandoned the struggle.

During the negotiations of surrender Colonel Hugh Wynne of Bodysgallen was held as hostage by the Cheshire forces. Two North Wales officers were among those in the city who signed the articles of surrender. These were Colonel John Robinson and Lieutenant-Colonel Peter Griffiths of Caerwys.

The elaborate articles—they numbered eighteen—included one which gave the garrison under Lord Byron freedom to march to Conway. 'The Welsh officers and soldiers shall have liberty to go to their own homes, all of

---

[120]*Phillips.* vol. 2. pp. 288-291.
[121]Ibid. vol. 2. p. 291.

them to have free quarters on the march, and twelve carriages, if they shall have occasion to use so many.'[122]

On February 3 the gallant defenders marched forth with the honours of war, the officers with horses and swords, the men bearing their arms.

The fall of Chester had a far-reaching effect on the Welsh counties. Hitherto the 'Parliamenteers'[123] had paid little attention to any of the strongholds except Hawarden and Holt but once the loyal city could no longer perform its tutelary task the northern shires lay open and unprotected. Triumphant Roundheads surged across the border and Major-General Mytton launched a campaign which was to place him among the war's successful generals.

The magnificent castle of Chirk was the first to be grasped. Here was no gallant resistance. John Watts, whom Charles had knighted a few months before, John Watts who characterised Archbishop Williams a traitor, slunk away, leaving the castle, well provisioned, to the care of Sir Thomas Myddelton's daughter. And Mytton held a receipt for a £200 bribe!

Thomas Malbon places the date as February 23, William Maurice considered it the 28. Was it in the hope of preventing this that Sir John Owen was ordered to rendezvous at Wrexham on February 23?[124] The Lord St Paul— his name is spelt variously—is a colourful and mysterious character. He fought valiantly in defence of Chester. On January 8 an agent brought the intelligence that Lord St Paul had reached Flint Castle 'privately, without any force.'

'Upon his going away a fire was made on ye top of Hawarden Castle to give them notice at Chester'[125]—that he was safely through the Parliamentary cordon. Lord St Paul was, as it transpired, on his way to Conway to organise a fresh attempt to relieve the city.

He escaped from Wales and was with Lord Astley when, on March 14, that veteran surrendered the last royal

[122]*Phillips.* vol. 2. pp. 294-297.
[123]A contemporary term.
[124]D.N.B.
[125]*Chester.* vol. XXV. p. 171.

army in the field with the prophetic observation: 'You have now done your work and may go play, unless you fall out among yourselves.' [126]

When Chester submitted, Hawarden's fate was inevitable, and its governor, Sir William Neale, having received royal permission, hauled down his flag on March 16.

The Parliamentarians were in the town of Ruthin as early as January 24—'most seasonable', Brereton informed the Speaker, 'for Ruthin Castle was so unprovided, as that we have now great hopes of reducing that strong castle.' The siege began about the beginning of March and occupied a matter of six weeks. The articles of surrender were signed on the 8th and the castle handed over on the 12th April. Writing to the Parliament Mytton admitted 'The reducing of this Castle of Ruthin hath cost me more time and ammunition than I expected when I first laid siege to it.' [127]

The articles were signed by John Raignolds, deputy governor. Of Captain Sword there is no mention; he may have lost his life in the siege.

There were good men and true in Denbigh Castle some eight miles away and they meant to make a last bid to aid their comrades in Ruthin. The day before the surrender, a party of horsemen rode out from Denbigh at dawn—sixty cavalrymen and thirty mounted firelocks—resolved to surprise Captain Richard Price's quarters, which were situated two miles from Ruthin—probably at Rhewl. Captain Price was vigilant; his scouts reported the Cavaliers' advance and the alarum was carried to Ruthin. Here Colonel John Carter was in charge of a horse guard, always on duty 'to secure the out-quarters' and frustrate any such attempt. With him was Captain Symkys of Mytton's own troop of horse. Circling the raiders the Parliamentary horse surprised the king's party within half a mile of their garrison, charged them, and claimed to have killed seven. In the pursuit forty horses were taken and a number of riders among whom were Captain Morgan of Golden Grove (after whom Morgan's Mount at Chester is named), Captain Hugh Morris, Captain

---

[126]*Rushworth.* vol. 6. p. 140.
[127]*Phillips.* Vol. 2. p. 301.

Wynne and Captain Pickering.[128] Colonel Salesbury disputed the figures asserting on his honour that one man only was slain.[129]

No sooner had Ruthin capitulated than Mytton pressed impatiently towards Denbigh. He apparently considered Holt Castle to be of nuisance value only and, having invested it, concentrated on his main objective which was Caernarvon Castle where Lord Byron (calling himself Field-Marshal-General of North Wales), had established his headquarters. Mytton dare not ignore powerful Denbigh but he so encompassed it that its defenders, even though they made numerous sorties, could not cut his line of communications. As the vanguard of Mytton's army advanced a party of Cavaliers disputed the way and slew a captain.

'They met with a rather warm reception from the garrison and were at first repulsed, with some loss and one commanding officer slain,' writes Williams. 'This compelled them to march on, or retreat towards Llandyrnog. But having again rallied, they returned to Whitchurch, where they lay encamped for several months, occupied in throwing up siege-works, and in constant skirmishes and sorties from the garrison who made descents upon their entrenchments and foraging parties.' [130]

As soon as road surface permitted, the heavy guns and mortars which had battered Chester into submission, were dragged towards Denbigh. One battery was placed on the south-western slope near the Myddelton ancestral home, Galch-hill, with the intention of breaching the castle on its most exposed side.[131] Another spot on which fire was concentrated was the Goblin Tower, part of the town wall which rises from the plain. A crescent shaped mound close to the tower base is to be seen in the grounds of Howells School. The concave side is towards the wall and it was doubtless thrown up by the Cavaliers to protect the founda-

[128]*Phillips.* vol. 2. pp. 301-303.
[129]*Newcome (Den.).* p. 73.
[130]*A.&M.* pp. 223-4.
[131]Ibid. 162.

-tion of the tower from the bombardment which scarred its upper masonry. A contemporary account of the attack on Denbigh Castle reads:

> 'There are mounts raised round about it, and approaches for battering a tower called the Goblin's Tower: hoping thereby to deprive them of the benefit of a well in that tower; which, can we attain, we may then soon expect the castle through want of water—they having but one well more, which is usually (as it is reported) dry in June or July every summer.' [132]

Mytton, having satisfied himself that Salesbury's five hundred defenders were safely encased in Denbigh's walls, ventured on a reconnaissance as far as Llanrwst, a bridgehead which the king's party had failed to seize despite talk of establishing a garrison there under Colonel John Thelwall. Their oversight proved costly. It is true that Lord Byron sent an eleventh hour order to Sir John Owen at Conway to destroy the bridge but by April 24 Mytton was already in possession. The general was entertained at Gwydir by the Wynns, and on leaving the following day he issued a warrant to Owen Wynn granting him protection 'upon pain of death.' [133]

Wynn's association with the enemy provoked Sir John Owen shortly after to drive away 200 of the Gwydir cattle —which proved acceptable to the castle larder at Conway.[134]

A contemporary pamphlet states that Mytton drew out of his leaguer at Denbigh 'a party of about 300 Horse and Foote, and led them in his own person, advancing neere Conway, a strong hold of the Enemies, neere which place they tooke 11 prisoners marching.' [135]

It is difficult to establish the exact moment when the erstwhile ardent servant of the king, Dr. John Williams, Archbishop of York, turned his episcopal coat, but it must have occurred about this time. Williams had retired to his

---

[132]*Phillips.* vol. 2. p. 307.
[133]*C.W.P.* 1770.
[134]Ibid. 2096-2099.
[135]*A bloody Fight at Blackwater*, London, June, 1646.

house at Penrhyn (once the home of the sea-dog, Piers Griffith) which stood on a site now occupied by Penrhyn Castle. He told Maurice Wynne at Gwydir in a letter written on April 29 that he had not been used unkindly hitherto, having stated that he kept his house 'neither against the King nor the Parliament but to prevent surprizalls.' [136]

One story is that the prelate was annoyed by Byron's predatory troopers and sent to Mytton for aid—help which was willingly given. The pamphlet already quoted states: 'Yes, my Lord of Yorke was very zealous to promote this worke, keeping his house Penryne a Garison against the Lord Byron for which he suffered many bitter invectives from the said Lord.' The account also states that the former Commissioner of Array, Sir William Williams, 'also was very forward to afford the Generall all accommodations fortifying also his house against the Lord Byron.'

The writer explains that the eleven prisoners were marching from Aberystwyth with a pass for Caernarvon which they had falsified and were heading for Conway.

> 'Two whereof were Irish which the General caused to be hanged immediately according to the Ordinance in that kinde.'
> 'From thence they advanced to Penrin, where the General and Officers were kindley entertained and feasted (being Wednesday the 29, of Aprill.).'

Mytton's advance was by way of the old Roman road through Bwlch-y-ddeufaen (the Pass of the Two Stones). By this time he must have been joined by a considerable force for he continued his advance towards Caernarvon . . . . 'where the enemy was ready to entertaine them, having lined their hedges, ditches, to obstruct their passage, and furnished the Subburbs with a great strength both of Horse and Foote.'

Evidently the small knoll known as the Twthill figured in the operations for the account continues: 'The General having viewed their condition, divided his Body into 2 parts,

---

[136] *C.W.P.* 2865.

leading one of them himselfe towards the high Rocke, and the Subburbs on the North-side of the Towne, where the chief strength of the Enemy lay, but the dispute contrived not long; for though the enemy came out furiously yet the gallant behaviour of that small party which the General (? commanded) speedily forced them from the hedges to the houses.' [137]

Another account states that the General laid the siege with exceeding difficulty. 'The enemy have made since the siege, which hath been now very nigh one month, two desperate sallies.' [138] During the first, the garrison lost seven or eight; the second cost them 17 prisoners, including a lieutenant and four more officers. Before the forces of the Parliament arrived Lord Byron 'burnt the suburbs, and sent Mr. Spicer, with a company of soldiers, for provision, who robbed and took all the cattle they found, and returned, but Spicer was taken.' [139]

William Maurice has his slight contribution to make to the situation: 'Towards the latter end of Aprill, Jo. Williams, Archbyshope of Yorke, yealded Penrhyn house to Generall Mytton, and assisted the Parlm in beseiging of Carnarvon, where ye Lo Byron had retreated for safety, after the rendition of West Chester.'

Whatever the cause Williams had now thrown in his lot with the victorious Parliamentarians; indeed, Mytton in a letter to London on April 30 reported that the prelate had abandoned the king's party.

It will be remembered that on the eve of war Sir Thomas Salusbury told Bulkeley of Baron Hill that in Caernarvonshire the Puritans 'bragged of a great party'. Royalist superiority had hitherto kept this beneath the surface but now that Mytton was hammering at the gates of Caernarvon and the archbishop had openly made his decision, many others followed suit. Squires who had served, perhaps with reluctance, on the Commission of Array, now turned against Byron, who, in any event, could hardly have been a wel-

---

[137] *A Bloody Fight at Blackwater.*
[138] *Phillips.* vol. 2. p.307.
[139] *Parry.* 362.

come guest, for his troopers ranged the countryside threatening all who refused contributions. In addition to Sir William Williams of Vaenol there was William Lloyd, later to be sheriff and sacrifice his life, Colonel Thomas Madryn, and Colonel Thomas Glynne of Glynllifon, elder brother of the famous parliamentary legal light, Serjeant John Glynne. It was Thomas Glynne 'who having great power in those parts did by his invitation prevaile much for the Generalls advance', and was, in the words of the pamphleteer 'God's principall Instrument.'

Caernarvon formerly obtained relief from the sea, but the invaders now had so many ships and boats off the coast that the besieged despaired of succour. They suffered from a great want of water.[140] About May 22 Mytton sent a second summons to surrender.

While the siege was in progress Mytton dispatched three commissioners, Colonel Roger Pope, Colonel John Jones of Maes-y-garnedd, and Thomas Edwardes, to Anglesey to negotiate for the surrender of the island. The Parliament attached so much importance to Anglesey that they instructed Mytton to offer a bribe of £2,000 for the island's submission.[140a] On June 1 Captain Stephen Rich with the armed Parliamentary vessels the *Rupert* and *Rebecca* anchored in Beaumaris roads awaiting a pass to proceed to Caernarvon.[141] The Parliamentary party were evidently active in Anglesey as Byron had to send to Viscount Bulkeley a warrant for the apprehension of Sir Robert Eyton, kt. of Beaumaris, whom he designated a spy, 'employed by the enemy to draw the inhabitants from their allegiance and to give intelligence to the Parliamentary forces.' A Royalist officer, Major David Lloyd, former mayor of Beaumaris, was also suspect.

Supporting Colonel Richard Bulkeley, Lord Bulkeley's heir, was the more experienced soldier, Lieut.-Colonel John Robinson, former governor of Holt Castle. With his home, Gwersyllt near Wrexham, in Parliamentary hands Robinson

---

[140]*Phillips.* vol. 2. p. 307.
[140a]*S.P.D.* p. 383.
[141]*C.W.P.* 1776.

transferred his service to Anglesey where he possessed a second house, Monachdy, on the rugged northern shore. Bulkeley complained to Captain Rich of the *Rebecca* in Friars road that his seamen had landed in the dead of night conveying arms and ammunition to the outpost at Aberlleiniog, known as Lady Cheadle's fort.[142]

While the commissioners were deliberately but successfully negotiating in Anglesey, Mytton was pressing home his attack on Caernarvon and on June 4 the mighty fortress capitulated. Byron's negotiating commissioners were Colonel Edward Vere, Colonel John Vane, and Lieut.-Colonel Disney. Mytton was represented by Colonel Thomas Glynne (soon to be made governor of captured Caernarvon), Colonel John Carter and Sergeant-Major Hierome Zanchy, who commanded Brereton's troop of horse and was a fighting-preacher. Under the articles Byron, the officers, and the gentlemen with their servants were granted leave to go to their homes or friends and they were allowed to make peace with the parliament or else go beyond the seas. Benefit of the articles was conferred upon Sir William Byron (another of the governor's brothers), Lieut.-Colonel John Robinson, Colonel Jeffrey Shakerley of Rowton Moor fame, Archdeacon Price and several others.

The surrender of Beaumaris Castle and Anglesey almost automatically followed on June 14, Colonel Bulkeley's negotiating commissioners being Lieut.-Colonel John Robinson, Dr. Robert Price and Major David Lloyd. All in the castle were to have General Mytton's best assistance to dispense with their past delinquency and the officers and gentlemen were to have four months in which to make their peace with the Parliament. The gentlemen might remove their own property from the castle but this did not include victuals, ammunition, artillery, or the muskets of the veteran trained bands.[143] Only five castles now remained—Denbigh,

---

[142]*C.W.P.* 1784.
[143]*Phillips.* vol. 2. pp. 312-313.

Flint, Rhuddlan, Conway and Holt, to which might be added isolated Harlech.

✿   ✿   ●

Flint was apparently closely besieged by May 22 which makes it difficult to account for the presence of Colonel Roger Mostyn at Gloddaeth on May 28. The governor of Flint was undoubtedly there for on that date he wrote to his uncle, Maurice Wynn at Gwydir, warning him to be on his guard against raids by Sir John Owen's troopers, adding that in Gloddaeth they were in continual danger from attacks by the Conway men.[144] Roger's familiarity with the district may have enabled him to break through the Parliamentary cordon when he learnt of the menace to his property. He was in Flint Castle during the protracted siege that hot summer for his uncle, Bulstrode Whitelock asserts that he 'held it out till all provisions, even to Horses, failing him, and then rendered it up upon honourable terms.'[145] Two days after the siege began 46 of his cavalrymen broke away and either surrendered or went to their homes.[146] With Roger in the castle was his father's brother, John Mostyn of Maesmynan and Tregarnedd, who was a Member of Parliament for Flint county until February 5, 1643, when he was 'disabled' (disqualified) for deserting the House and being in the King's quarters.

The articles of surrender were signed on August 20. The castle surrendered on the 24, the governor, officers and gentlemen being allowed to go to their homes and to have six months in which to make their peace with the Parliament. Soldiers were permitted to march out with the honours of war and go to their homes, 'Colonel Mytton to use his best endeavours with the Parliament on behalf of Colonel Mostyn, the Governor, and Mr. John Mostyn.'[147] When the

---

[144]*C.W.P.* 1775 & 2866.
[145]*Memorials.*
[146]*Phillips.* vol. 2. p. 308.
[147]Flints. H.S. *Journal.* 1916-17. pp. 85-6.

castle surrendered Colonel Mostyn was only twenty-two years old. Impoverished, he was forced to dwell for a time in a farm-house on his estate but his loyalty remained unimpaired and he continued to work for the House of Stuart.

There must have been fierce fighting in Flint town. The description penned by John Taylor, the Water Poet, six years later depicts a place devoid of industry or accommodation, scarred and stunned by the misfortune which had befallen it. How different from the day four years before when young Roger with high aspirations raised fifteen hundred men for his king in twelve hours!

Now, Roundhead riders roamed the familiar roads. The stillness of a green countryside was disturbed by the dusty trampling of marching musketeers as 'rebels' forced their unwelcome way across the broad acres of royalist estates, and labouring gun-teams hauled culverins along leafy lanes to turn their ominous mouths against Flintshire ramparts.

The operations before Rhuddlan remain obscure. The governor, Colonel Gilbert Byron, was summed up by Archbishop Williams in a single caustic comment—'lately married and very indulgent to his lady'.

Rhuddlan was obviously more vulnerable than mighty Denbigh. The probability is that Mytton refrained from sacrificing lives in a spectacular assault when starvation would accomplish the task. The siege began in May; by the end of July Gilbert Byron surrendered. The attackers, thus released, swelled the ranks of their comrades before Denbigh's defiant walls.

CHAPTER TEN

By August Mytton was free to turn his attention to Conway. Thanks to the earlier exertions of Archbishop Williams the castle was in good repair and equipped with cannon. The normal garrison had been strengthened by men who arrived from surrendered fortresses. Sir Thomas Eyton of Eyton, Salop, was in the castle for his name appears as compounding on the Conway articles for his delinquency. Colonel John Whitley, a younger brother of Colonel Roger Whitley, was killed while defending Conway town.

One can only assume the composition of the force in Conway but a memorandum prepared after the surrender of Chester in February might furnish clues. In this Archbishop Williams inquired whether entertainment should be accorded, 200 foot and some gentlemen on horseback, 50 horsemen from Holt Castle who arrived under Lord St. Paul, and 80 of Lord Byron's men. In addition there were 100 men from Ireland and 90 from Beeston Castle and Latham house, 'generally commended for their carriage' (as might be expected). There were also 70 of Lord Byron's troopers who had taken foot-arms under Captain Robert Pugh of the Penrhyn Creuddyn family.[148] Though several months had passed since these words were penned it is probable that a number of these warriors remained in Conway. Bishop Hacket might contemptuously observe that 'the Conweiians would as soon fight for a May-poll as Sir John Owen', but the garrison gave proof of their resolution.

Archbishop Williams must have chafed under the indignity of being turned out of the castle[149] for when the attack was planned he readily participated despite his sixty odd years, and for so doing sustained a wound in the neck. Mytton's men had apparently been observing Conway since June though nothing in the nature of an assault was

---

[148]*C.W.P.* 1763.
[149]"Dr. Williams is no little vexed that Owen hath put such a trick upon him". (*Phillips*, vol. 2. p. 328).

attempted. The attack is vividly portrayed in a pamphlet printed on August 19, 1646.[150]

'On Saturday, the 8th of this instant, General Mytton returning to his military employment at Conway Castle (called) a Council of War, to which was joined the grand advice of Doctor Williams, sometime Archbishop of York, where he represents unto them his intentions, concerning the surprisal of the town of Conway, together with the former order for the managing of that service. It was concluded by all to be feasible, though full of doubt and hazard, and not to be effected without much loss, yet they resolved to use their best skill; and endeavour to commend the success and blessing to God. Resolute and approved men of his own horse and foot were employed, preparations of grenadoes and ladders made ready, and provisions. The service thus prosecuted and effected.

'Capt. Simkis was appointed to give and continue an alarm to the town on the North side; that while the enemy that were upon guard advanced themselves to defend and secure that part of the town, Major Elliot on the South side, and Capt. Camburs and Capt. Gethin in two other places, with three select companies of resolute men, might as they were ordered make their advantage of that opportunity . . . Such was the resolution and gallantry of the soldiers, that though some were knocked down and crushed with horses, others cast off the ladders (which were ten yards high, and yet proved a yard and a half too short), that they renewed the action and drawing up over the other by the arm,[151] till a considerable company were got over; which being done they fell into the town, surprised the main-guard, killed a corporal and a gentleman there, wounded many, took a major, one Capt. Wynne, an old cowdriver, four lieutenants, four ensigns, twenty-two soldiers of fortune, and fifty townsmen in arms. Many [Irish] were commanded to be tied back to back, and to be cast overboard, and sent by water to their own country. There was one great gun taken, 200 arms,

---

[150]*Phillips*. vol. 2. pp. 325-327.
[151]An ambiguity in the printing.

ammunition answerable, wine, corn, and victuals good store, and considerable booty for the soldiers. The guards being sent for, the town secured, and all things quiet, the General sent this summons for the surrender of the castle namely:—

Sir,

I cannot but be sensible of the misery you have brought upon your country by holding this town and castle from the obedience of the King and Parliament. Now it hath pleased God to give this town into our hands I can do no less than put you in mind, that your holding of the castle can produce no other probable effect than the effusion of Christian blood, and the ruin of your country. And by what authority you do it I am ignorant: the King being come into our quarters, and made known unto you that he is not able to relieve you. I cannot omit to tell you what a desperate condition you will bring yourself and [your] estate into, if you persist in your way but a few days. I do, therefore, summon you to deliver the castle into my hands for the service of the Parliament, and expect your answer within two hours.

Your servant,

Conway, August 9th, 1646.   Tho: Mytton.

To this Sir John Owen from the castle replied:—

'Sir,

I received yours yesterday, and this day I send you mine. I wonder you should tax me with bringing misery upon this country, which my conscience tells me I am free of, especially in doing my endeavour to hold it in obedience to his Majesty.

'Now you have gotten the town, I expect no other title from you than of the castle, which title I will maintain with my life. For the effusion of Christian blood, far be it from my heart, only I must seek to defend myself and those that are with me. As for the ruin of the country let the blood of those that lost it fall upon them that were the contrivers of it. I free you and yours. And if you would know by what authority I hold this place, I have formerly given you an answer. You writ that the

105

King was in the Parliament's quarter. I believe he was never further from them; and withal you believe he hath made it known unto me he is not able to relieve me: this point I doubt very much. You tell me a desperate condition I will bring myself and estate, in persisting in not yielding to your desires. I can be nothing bettered unless you have an absolute power from the Parliament. As for your summons, I shall hold this castle as long as it pleaseth God, for his Majesty. Yet, if you shall accept of such conditions as I shall propound, which shall be honourable for us both, I will be content to treat with you only,

And rest, Sir, your servant,

J. Owen.

Mytton replied that he was prepared to consider these proposals whereupon Sir John asked for three days in which to prepare them. They were not received by August 12. The attack on the castle was resumed.

A strange situation must have existed within the ancient walls of the Edwardian borough. Roundheads lodged in the houses and patrolled the streets. Cavaliers looked down from the towering ramparts and doubtless took shots at any incautious Parliamentarian who strayed within range. The archbishop could not have been severely wounded. He celebrated the capture of his native town by preaching in the parish church in which he was christened. He chose a right fighting text from the first verse of the 144 Psalm: *'Blessed be the Lord my Strength, which teacheth my hands to war and my fingers to fight.'*

The House of Commons was informed that 'Conway holds out. Their flesh is spent, corne and Beere they have in store.' By September 14 Mytton reported 'the rendering of Conway goes on well.' Then he passed over the conduct of the siege to Colonel Jones. By October 13 it was reported that 'General Mytton had planted two pieces of cannon (very near) for batteries.' [152]

Doubtless these were on the slope above the Woodlands

---

[152]Prelate-at-Arms by Norman Tucker.

on the south side of the Gyffin Stream. Edmund Hyde Hall thought so when he examined the terrain in 1809.

'Some testimonies to this attack are still to be seen in the balls (three-pound shots) occasionally found, and in the battered appearance of the south wall where the town connects itself with the castle. Upon the opposite bank the line of the battery may be traced, though it has been smoothed down in a great degree by the labour of the plough.' [153]

When the castle was taken it was found to possess seven pieces of ordnance and six barrels of gunpowder, so it may be assumed that the bombardment met with a spirited response. The recent researches of Mr. A. J. Taylor have thrown fresh light on the siege. After Colonel John Carter was made governor of the captured fortress his expenses included money for repairing platforms for the great guns in the castle, and also for mounting and fitting those guns. Additional costs were for repairing the three drawbridges 'that were shattered and spoyled in the time of the siege.' [154]

There are still unanswered questions. Did the archbishop dwell in his own house? Was Plas Mawr used by the victors as their headquarters and were the coloured plaster escutcheons and crests whitewashed at this period? Who were the 'other Welch' who assisted the archbishop in the assault? 'Captain Wynne' was the only prisoner mentioned by name which suggests he was well known. Might he have been a Wynne of Plas Mawr? Robert Wynne, the deputy mayor whose tomb is in the chancel of Conway church, was alive at the time.

Conway must be pictured with battle-smoke curling grey amid the yellowing leaves, and the air trembling to the roar of cannon as red-coated soldiers of the New Model Army made a garish splash of colour in the sombre streets. It was November 18 before Sir John Owen and his men marched out with the honours of war.

---

[153] *Hyde Hall.* p. 65.
[154] *'Conway Castle and Town Walls.* Ministry of Works' Official Guide. p. 9.

The three months' siege which Conway endured cannot be compared in its intensity with that of Denbigh. It was, nonetheless, a considerable achievement on the part of Sir John Owen to withstand so long, particularly when the town itself was in his enemy's keeping. The so-called 'hanging tower' on the south side of the castle is traditionally said to have collapsed in the 18th century, because residents took too many of its stones for building their walls. This may well be so, but it is highly probably that in the first instance the foundations were weakened by Mytton's bombardment.

A quaint sidelight on the siege has survived. The Parliamentary commander, evidently as an inducement to the garrison to come to terms in November, wrote:

'Conwaie, 10 of 9ber, 1646.
'I promise that euerie musquetiere in the castle of Conwaie shall haue Ten shillings a peece when they laie down theire armes upon Fridaie.
                                                    Thos. Mytton.'

Sir John retired to his home at Clenennau, impoverished but honoured—and inwardly resolved to draw the sword again on the first opportunity. As might be expected he was heavily fined.

It will be recollected that one of Archbishop William's conditions for supporting Mytton in his attack on Conway was that the valuables stored in the castle should be returned to their owners. Hacket asserts: 'Mytton kept the Castle and kept his word too, to let the owners divide the goods among themselves to which they had title and could prove it.'

CHAPTER ELEVEN

THERE is a tendency to regard the Civil War in terms of land warfare overlooking the effect of maritime operations, yet the entire issue was influenced by the navy's early espousal of the Parliamentary cause. When 1642 dawned the king had three vessels in the Irish Sea. These, based on Dublin, were the twenty-gun ship *Swan* and the armed merchantmen *Phoenix* and *Confidence*. Early in the year the *Phoenix* was cast away mysteriously on the Great Orme leaving only the *Swan* and *Confidence* to fly his Majesty's war flag in these waters. If the entire story of the exploits of these gallant little craft could be written it would provide a saga of the sea. The king's ship was commanded by Captain John Bartlett, formerly a Dublin merchant, while Captain Tom Bartlett was skipper of the appropriately-named *Confidence*. John was the senior but whether these two loyal sea-dogs were father and son, or two brothers has not yet been established. Before hostilities commenced Tom Bartlett was entrusted with the unenviable task of carrying Parliamentary commissioners from Dublin to London river in the *Confidence*. To his chagrin he was detained but managed to gain his freedom and bring the *Confidence* back to Dublin in time to plough the waves of the St. George's Channel on many risky passages. Again and again the daring *Confidence* ran the Parliamentary blockade bearing dispatches or carrying men and munitions to Beaumaris or Conway.

In January 1643 'Captaine Baldwyn Wake, a captaine of the late King's, coming to harbour in Bewmares in co. Anglesey with a Fleete of 14 Sayle of Shippes threatened to spoyle and ruinate the sayd Towne of Bewmares and Countie of Anglisey unless hee should be supplied with victualles and other necessaries.' [155]

The reason for Wake's presence and the nature of his activities are alike wrapped in mystery but he seems to have made little use of his opportunities. He was in the vicinity

---

[155]Anglesey Field Club & Ant. Soc., *Tr.*, 1948, p. 65.

on December 7, 1643, as a letter written to Mr. Michael
Lewis at Beaumaris on that date indicates.

'Mr. Michael Lewes. There being a present necessity of
vittualing Captain Wake, and the other shippes now
with him in Chester watter, and understandinge that
you have 80-100 Barrells of Beefe ready salted and fitt
ffor Shippinge at Bewmarys wee have thought to make
lese of 16,000 weight of the Beefe ffor him and wee doe
undertake to satisfie you fforthwᵗʰ. Accordinge to such
rates, as shalbe reasonably Agreed on by Capt. Chedle &
your Selfe, no Corne or other provisions of vittuals, and
this beinge ffor the present use of the ffleet wee make
noe doubt that you will readily Comply with our order
and desire, soe wee bidd you hartily ffarewell herein,
your very loveinge ffriends,
ARTHUR CAPELL,
JOHN BYRON,
NICH: BYRON,
AB: SHIPMAN,
OR: BRIDGMAN.
Chester Decᵇᵉʳ 7th. 1643.' [156]

The date suggests that Wake and his vessels may have
participated in the expedition which resulted in the landing
of the English-Irish army a couple of weeks before. There is
no account of any naval action off the coast as would almost
inevitably have occurred had Wake been in the vicinity that
summer when a small Parliamentary squadron under
Captain Danske put in an appearance. The sight of the first
'enemy' warships off Anglesey caused consternation among
the Royalist inhabitants. Their anxiety is reflected in a
letter[157] written by Dr. William Griffith of Carreglwyd, to
Thomas Bulkeley of Baron Hill, the Lord Lieutenant.

'Truely wee are shrewdly affrighted in these naked parts
by three men of Warre whereof two anchor'd neare
land all day yesterday and last night at a place called
Yr Wylfa three miles from mee, the third at Holyhead

[156]U.C.N.W. *Baron Hill MSS.* 5367.
[157]Now in the library of the University College of North Wales.

where it still remaineth, but that being farther from mee, and come in since the other two, I cannot give you any certaine account of it, but that it is a tall vessell bearing diverse Peeces of Ordnance . . . ffor the other two as soon as I heard of their anchoring and continuance in a place unusual for shipps of that burden, I went thither in the evening yesterday to enforme my self the best I could of them, and to persuade my neighbours to keep a good watch in respect of them last night, and truly I believe all the musketts of these parts attended there last night; but surely this morning they weighed Anchors and I believe you heare of them about Beaumares before this time.

'All wee could learne of them here by some that were sent aboard the greater of them was that they were men of warre full of men and Ammunition; in the greater were seene 6 pieces of ordinance ready mounted, and 8 unmounted, and the people that went aboard it, saw 40 or 50 men in one roome at two tables at dinner, what further company there was in the ship they could not see. There was one Welshman of their company with whom our men conferred, and who told them that they were sent into these parts by the Earl of Warwick to secure theis Coaste from some Dunkirkes[158] that lye in these Irish Seas. I fear that you will soon apprehend their errand concearnes us more nearly; and had they not departed from us very timely today, I was resolved to have sent a dispatch to you to advertise what unwellcome neighbours wee had . . . I may add that they were inquisitive to learn of our men, how matters stood between King and Parliament, which I conceave was but to fish their disposition towards them. The Welshman of their company would not tell what county of Wales hee was, neither would hee tell us theire Capt's name. They were seene yesterday before they came to the aforesaid place of Anchorage to sound our shores as they went for 6 or 7 miles . . . The 2 shipps I wrote of wee guess to bee, the one of about 120 Tunns, and the lesser of about 100 Tunns, the lesser seemed to be as full of men as the other.' [159]

---

[158]Pirates from Dunkirk.
[159]*Baron Hill MSS.* 5368.

Before the Parliamentary ships arrived the Bartletts had been stealing across the Irish Sea with supplies for the king's forces. Sir William Brereton early in 1643 wrote: 'Captain Barkely (sic) who commands the Kings pinnace, the *Swan*, is very officious to the Commissioners of Array, and hath promised them two pieces of ordnance to guard Chester. It is said the Comers have given him £500 or £1,000. If some speedy care be not taken to prevent him, he may do very much mischief.' [160]

The Bartletts were joined by the *Griffon* and also by Captain Lloyd in the '*Swan* frigott', a small vessel, carrying only a few guns, which Mr. Aled Eames considers served as a tender to the great ship whose name she bore. In January 1644 the Parliament dispatched a squadron of five ships and a frigate to watch the coast of Ireland. The admiral was Captain Richard Swanley who flew his flag in the *Leopard Regis*, with Captain William Smith as vice-admiral in the *Swallow*. The remaining vessels were: *Prosperous*, Captain Nicholas Gottenby; *Providence*, Captain William Swanley; *Leopard* merchant, Captain John Guilson; and *Crescent* frigate, Captain Peter Whittey (or Whitley). There were also 'two Liverpool vessels.'

The magnificent harbour of Milford Haven became their base. Here, in addition to capturing two Royalist ships, they reduced a fort and assisted in land operations for which the admiral and vice-admiral were voted gold chains by an appreciative parliament. They cruised north on a number of occasions. Lord Ormonde had occasion to complain that he could not send Colonel Francis Trafford and 300 men to Anglesey because of two Parliamentary ships and a frigate anchored off the coast of Dublin. Again he wrote: 'The ships imployed by the Parliament as it were blocked up these coasts, some riding upon the point of Ayre near Mosson (Mostyn) betwixt Beaumarice and Chester. The same lately took away seven barques with much scandall and insolency out of the very port of Holyhead, they being bound hither with provisions.'

[160]*Chester.* vol. XXV. p. 38

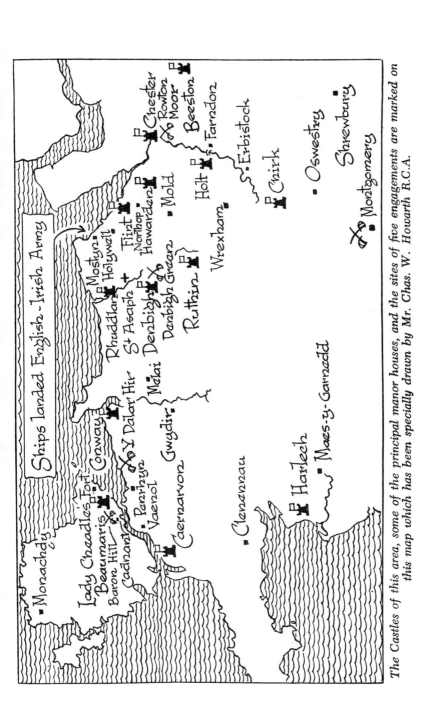

The Castles of this area, some of the principal manor houses, and the sites of five engagements are marked on this map which has been specially drawn by Mr. Chas. W. Howarth R.C.A.

Ships landed English ~ Irish Army

Monachdy
Lady Chaadlas Fort
Beaumaris
Baron Hill
Cadnant
Penrhyn
Vaenol
Caernarvon
Y Dalar Hir
Gwydir
Conway
Clenannau
Harlech
Maes-y-Garnedd
Mōlai
Denbigh
Danbigh Green
Ruthin
Mostyn
Holywell
Rhuddlan
St Asaph
Flint
Northop
Hawarden
Mold
Wrexham
Holt
Chester
Rowton Moor
Beeston
Farndon
Erbistock
Chirk
Oswestry
Shrewsbury
Montgomery

This was in May 1644. One record tells of Caernarvon being captured by Swanley's fleet but confirmatory evidence is lacking. Towards the end of the war Swanley was so confident that he offered to take Dublin if he could have his force strengthened. He was hated by the Royalists as 'a bloody mariner' who flung soldiers from Ireland overboard bidding them swim back to their native land.

From 1643 onwards Archbishop Williams established a service between Conway and Dublin which was as regular as weather and watch-ships permitted.

'Let Captain Bartlett bring hither cannon and ammunition and to trust them at Conway,' he wrote to Ormonde. 'The cannon shall be safe and the ammunition paid for. I have likewise presumed to be a humble suitor unto your excellency for the greater of some four or five skiffs or frigates which lie unused, and two pieces of ordnance to be used in her.'

He suggested that Captain Bartlett towed the vessel to Beaumaris 'ready to serve your Excellency from time to time.' Some time before this the archbishop complained that there were but three or four fisher-boats along the North Wales coast.

The manner in which Ormonde secured, with great difficulty, sufficient ships to transport Irish regiments across to aid the king is part of the history of the Civil War. Less known are the passages of the individual ships but casual references to Captain Bartlett or Captain Lloyd indicate that their vessels frequently arrived at Beaumaris and Conway with powder and stores.

A record in April 1645 tells of one of Bartlett's ships coming into Dublin harbour with prizes taken off the Scottish coast, but so battered was his vessel that it would take a considerable time to re-rig her.

It is difficult today to imagine Chester as the chief port for Ireland. This extract proves that vessels could sail right up to the city in Civil War days.

'My bote (the *Rebecca*) was yesterday at Chester and gave the Towne and Alarum and shott in to ye Towne with one of our Gunnes.' [161] So wrote Captain Stephen Rich on May 18, 1645. The enterprising captain proposed to Sir William Brereton that he might that night capture a king's ship which was moored off Flint Castle. He asked for more boats 'to attempt designs worth note.'

As the siege of Chester intensified Brereton ordered that a vessel should guard the approach to the river day and night 'lest provisions should be brought in by water to the besieged. A woman spy at Conway had reported that a vessel carrying 300 measures of wheat, thirty flitches of bacon and '4 fatt Beeves' had left Conway and reached Mostyn but had to turn back on account of adverse winds. The vessel had on board in addition to her crew, thirty soldiers, as it was planned to capture the *Robbin*—evidently one of Brereton's watch-ships. Rich's vessel was furnished with two cannon and twelve musketeers. He assured Sir William that his own pinnace in addition to another vessel would coast up and down night and day. Later he reported: 'I have three nimble vessels fitted inne with four peeces of ordnance, one with two pieces, besides my shallops.' [162] When a last attempt to relieve Chester was being made in January 1646 the king's party had several vessels at Conway and Rhuddlan laden with corn, bacon and other provisions.

The strength of the little Parliamentary fleet did not however suit Colonel Chidley Coote who complained to Brereton that if Chester was to be protected they must have something better than 'a stinkeinge boate or two yt are not able to doe any good.' [163]

When Chester was captured and the Parliament forces advanced into the interior of Wales Captain Rich with the *Rebecca* and *Rupert* followed along the coast ready to co-operate. In June they were in Beaumaris roads where General Mytton issued a pass for them to proceed up the Menai Straits to Caernarvon. While at Beaumaris the crews apparently landed and Captain Rich was charged with a breach of the peace negotiations—which he stoutly denied.

[161]*Chester.* vol. XXV. p. 104.
[162]Ibid. p. 166.
[163]Ibid. p. 82n.

All hope of Caernarvon being relieved from the sea was abandoned because the Parliament had 'so many boats and ships.' [164]

From the Royalist point of view the sea struggle ended in tragedy. The gallant *Swan* at the very close of the first war was captured by Parliamentary seamen while most of her crew were ashore in Dublin.

[164]*Phillips.* vol. 2. p. 307. For further details see Sir Frederick Rees' *Studies in Welsh History*, and Mr. Aled Eames' article in the Caerns. H.S. *Tr.*, 1955, on *Sea Power and Caernarvonshire.*

CHAPTER TWELVE

DURING the close siege of Denbigh which lasted from April to October letters were periodically exchanged between the two commanders. All were couched in courteous terms, Mytton endeavouring to convince Salesbury of the futility of prolonging the struggle; the doughty governor steadfastly maintaining that until the king gave him leave he would not surrender his trust.

The first of these letters was dispatched by Mytton on the eve of the capture of Ruthin.

'Sir,—I can noe less than put you in mind of the losse of christian blood, the undoing of this country, and the retarding of the work of reformation in these parts (soe happily by God's blessing) not only began, but in great measure perfected in most parts of this kingdome, that you soe much cause, and will be deeply guilty of, if you persiste in your way, of your forcibly keeping this castle of Denbigh from being reduced to the obedience of the king and parliament, having no hopes of reliefe. 'I do therefore hereby summon you to deliver into my hands the castle of Denbigh for the use of the king and parliament, upon Monday next, by nine of the clock in the morninge; assuring you that you may have better conditions both for yourselfe and the rest of the castle with you, if you refuse not this my first summons, than eyther you or they can expect hereafter if you doe refuse it, and thereby cause mee to desire the parliament that the whoall charge of this seige may for the saving of this poor exhausted countrey from ruyne bee maintayned out of your and there estates, which will certenly be prosecuted by him who rather desires to bee unto you, as heretofore,

Your ould friend and servant,

Tho. Mytton.

Denbigh town, 17 April, 1646.

I expect your answer by 9 of the clocke too-morrow morning.'

Colonel Salesbury replied: —

In nomine Jesu
18th Aprilis, 1646.

'I am sorry to see the ruine of my in'ocent native countrey, for there loyalty to there king, and sensible of the effusion of christian blood, but upon whose account that which is, or shall be spilt in your attempt to force this castle from mee, being our king's own house—entrusted to mee, unsought, both by his Majestie's commission and verbal com'and, I will leave it to the Highest Judge;—and, in answere to your summons, I will say no more then that, with God's assistance, I doe resolve to make good this place till I receive our king' com'and and warrant of my discharge —to whome, under God, wee all are tyed by common allegiance; and, when I shall have need of relief, I shall undoubtedly expect it from my merciful God, who knows the justness of my cause, and soe rest

Your ould friend and servant,
William Salesbury.' [165]

General Mytton was not the only person to appeal to the governor to abandon resistence. On May 8 a petition signed by forty-seven residents was sent to the castle, begging the governor to avoid spilling Christian blood and ruining many poor and rich by the continuance of the siege. It was evidently sponsored by the Member for Denbigh, Simon Thelwall, who had returned from South Wales where he had served as a colonel of horse. His name headed the list of what was known as 'The Bumpkin's Petition'.

Salesbury's reply was addressed to 'Cosin Thelwall— and the rest of the subscribers.' He wrote: —

'How I became interested in this place and command is very well knowne to the best of you; and with what moderation I have since managed it doth clerely appeare by the exhausting of my own estate for the supply of this castle (but what hath bin plundered from mee by the parliament forces) to avoyde any pressure upon the country; who cannot in justice com-

---

[165]*Newcome (Denbigh).* pp. 77-80.

playne, if the practice of other garrisons be impartially looked upon; and if by the advance of this force, your condition be rendered so deplorable as you mention, I am confident I shall stand acquitted before God and every good man; seeing all I do is in mayntenance of my allegiance and in persuance of the trust imposed in mee by MY KING (whom you doe not vouchsafe to take notice of)'.

He told them he could not see how matters would be improved by his surrender seeing that there were other castles of no less strength still under the king's command. He signed himself 'the king's loyall subject.' [166]

Once Caernarvon and Beaumaris were in the Parliament's hands Mytton again summoned Salesbury to surrender, this time on June 24 but with no better result. Salesbury retorted that what Caernarvon and Beaumaris did was no affair of his, he intended to continue to hold Denbigh for the king.

'As for the ruine of this innocent countrey, I am hartily sorry, that soe noble a gentleman, soe generally beeloved as yourself, of soe antient, and soe worthey a stocke, should bee made the prime actor therein.' [167]

Salesbury asked permission to send two gentlemen to the king to learn his pleasure. This Mytton was compelled to refuse as Parliament had directed that no such concession should be granted.

Conway town having been taken Mytton tried another summons, this time on August 30. 'I hope you will not make your countrey so miserable, in persisting any longer in houlding out this castle,' he wrote.

Again heading his reply '*In nomine Jesu*', Salesbury answered: —

'Sir, I shall ever acknowledge your curtesies, tho' unable to requite.—For the condition of our king and his kingdomes, if God have soe disposed, blessed be his

---

[166]*Newcome (Denbigh).* pp. 84-86.
[167]Ibid. p. 90.

name and welcome bee his will. In my answere to your second summons I desired your consent to send a gentleman or two to our king, to knowe his pleasure; but I received noe answere from you therein as yeat; the same desire I doe now second, being confident I shall speed, as others, who had the like granted from you; expecting your answere,

I rest, your servant,

William Salesbury.

'Sir,—I doe returne, per this Drume, Sir John Trevour's letter and the Diurnall.' [168]

Mytton in reply assured Salesbury that he had received a command from the Parliament not to suffer anyone to go to the king 'upon any pretence whatever'.

By this time it was evident that the troops which besieged such strongholds as Flint and Rhuddlan had now swelled the ranks of the besiegers for Salesbury in his reply, sent the same night (August 31), began:

'The coming of more forces to beseige this place will noe way move my resolution; who preferre noe ende to the acquitting myself like an honest man in that trust which my king hath committed to mee, which I am fully satisfied can never be done before my king receave an accompt of my proceedings (and without that, to deale freely with you) I have such an engagement upon mee, that I will not entertayne any overture of this nature;—and since I must beeleeve that your hands are tyed up, yeat I am so much concerned in this business, that I must apply myself to other means in that perticular for my satisfaction; which will take up some time; and if I must quit the place, I professe, I had rather you had the honour of it, than any other person in England, of your party; tho' give me leave to tell you, that the addition of a new force, bee the consequence what it will, will but add to my honour which is all I have now left to care for.

'I remayne your servant,

'Ult. Augti, 1646.   William Salesbury.' [169]

[168]Ibid. pp. 93-94.
[169]Ibid. pp. 96-97.

A message was entrusted by the governor to one of the loyal Thelwalls who managed to get through the enemy's lines and ride to the king in Newcastle with the following message: —

'*In nomine Jesu*.
'May it please your Majesty,
'I have presumed to make my humble address to you by this gentleman, Mr. Eubull Thelwall, to let your Majesty understand that this castle hath now for severall months byne closely besieged; what matter of action hath in that time happen'd, I humbly refere your Majesty to his relation, wherein I do beseech your Majesty to give him creddit; praying for your Majesty's health and happiness,
'I remayne,
   'Your Majestie's loyall subject,
     'William Salesbury.'

The king replied from Newcastle on September 13.

'Coronell Salesbury,
I hartely thank you for your loyall constancie, and assure you, that whensoever it shall please God to enable me to show my thankfullness to my friends, I will particularly remember you. As for your answer, I refer you to thease messengers, to whom I have clearly declared my minde; commend me to all my friends,
'So I rest,
   'Your most assured friend,
     Charles R.

The messengers bore the following warrant: —

'TO OUR TRUSTY AND WELL-BELOVED COLONEL WILLIAM SALESBURY, GOVERNOR OF THE CASTLE OF DENBIGH, IN WALES.
CHARLES R.

'Whereas, Wee have resolved to comply with the desires of our parliament in every thing which may bee for the good of our subjects, and leave noe means unassayed for removing all difference betwixt us—therefore wee have thought fitt, the more to evidence the reality of our intentions of sittling a happy and firm

121

peace, to authorize you upon honourable conditions, to quit, and surrender the castle of Denbigh, entrusted to you by us, and to disband all the forces under your commands; for which your soe doeing this shall bee your warrant.

'Given at Newcastle, the 14th of Sept. 1646.' [170]

More than a month passed before the garrison marched out and it is difficult to account for this lapse of time. Archdeacon Richard Newcome, from whose *History of the Town of Denbigh* the above correspondence is extracted, quotes the *Memoranda* of Wm. Morris for Sept. 28, 1646:

'Mr. William Salusbury of Rûg, after he hadd sente to the king to shew in what case the countrey stood and what misery they suffered by reason of the leaguer, and also how his souldiers in the castle were infected with divers diseases, was commanded by the king, and delivered up the castle to them upon the 26th Oct.' [171]

Williams states that the troops under Salesbury engaged the Parliamentarians in constant skirmishes and, in frequent sorties, descended upon their entrenchments and attacked their foraging parties. Details of one such happening have been preserved. Newcome quotes from 'MSS Memoranda in the possession of the heir of Llwyn.' This reads:

'Edward Wynn, 4th son of Edward Wynn, the only son of Maurice Wynn of Gwydir and Catherine of Beren, by Blanch his wife, daughter of John Vychan of Blaen y Cwm, was captain of a company of foot in Denbigh castle in the service of Charles the First, was wounded in a sally made by the said garrison against the beseigers under Sir (*sic*) John Carter, and in three days after died of his wounds, and was interred with military honours at Llanrhaiadr, being conducted as far as Ystrad Bridge, where he had three vollies, thence taken by a party of the Oliverians, who likewise conducted him to his grave after the same manner.' [172]

---

[170]Ibid. pp. 100-103.
[171]Ibid. p. 103.
[172]Ibid. p. 106.

Captain Wynn's tomb, a raised slab, is conspicuous in the churchyard in front of the east window. The inscription may still be read:

'Here lyeth ye Body of Capt Edward Wynne 4th son of Edwd Wynne. He dy'd in the defence of Denbigh Castle when besieged by Oliver Cromwell's army.'

Mention of Cromwell's name is misleading; he never fought in North Wales. Carter was not knighted until March, 1658[173], and was again knighted by Charles 11 at the Restoration.

Williams writes: 'On the way to Whitchurch is a place still called *Captain Bridge*, where tradition tells us a great battle was fought, and where a captain belonging to the garrison fell.' [174]

No bridge is to be seen at the spot now. The stream has diminished to a rivulet and is carried by a culvert under the Ruthin road.

In their report prepared about May 22, Lieutenant-Colonel George Twisleton, Lieutenant-Colonel Thomas Mason and Captain Richard Price described the governor as 'a verie wilful man.' Events confirmed their opinion. It had been a tedious siege. Williams, writing in 1856, states that 'Cannon-balls have frequently been dug up about the Castle, but they are mostly eight-pounders, and none, we believe, exceed 32. lb.' [175]

The articles of capitulation were signed upon October 14.[176] Mytton's commissioners were Colonel Simon Thelwall, M.P., Lieutenant-Colonel George Twisleton, Lieutenant-Colonel Thomas Mason, Roger Hanmer, Esq., Thomas Edwardes, Esq. (who also served as a commissioner with Colonel Mason at the Beaumaris surrender), Captain Robert Farrar and Nathaniell Barnett, clerk to the commissioners.

Colonel Salesbury's commissioners were: Lieutenant-Colonel (Peter) Griffiths (of Caerwys), Colonel Wynne

[173]C.W.P. 2151.
[174]A.&M. p. 228.
[175]A.&M. p. 229.
[176]S.P.D. pp. 234-237.

(probably of Bodysgallen), Major Francis Manley of Erbistock, Major Reynalds (probably the governor of Ruthin), John Eaton, Esq., John Thelwall, Esq., and Kenrick Eyton, Esq.

The articles, 16 in number, are too detailed to be reproduced in full[177] but some extracts may serve,

'No. 2. That Coll. William Salusbury, gouern[r] of ye towne and castle of Denbigh, wth his servants, and all that to him belongs, and all officers and souldiers of horse and foote, as well reformed officers and voluntere souldiers as others, and all other officers with theire seuants, and all yt appaynes to them, shall march out of ye towne and castle of Denbigh, w[th] theire horses, and armes proportionable to theire p[r]snt or past com'ands, flying colours, drums, beatinge, matches light at both ends, bullet in the mouth; eu[r]y souldier to have 12 chardges of powder, match and bullet p'portionable, w[th] bag and bagage p'perly to them belonginge; and all p'sons of quality clergymen, and gentlemen, w[th] theire seuants, horses and armes, in like manner w[th] bag and bagage, and all goodes to them p'perly belonginge to any place with[n] X miles, such as the gou[r]nor shall make choyce of; where, in regard ye king hath noe armie in the fielde, or garrison vnbeseidged, to march to; the com'on souldiers shall laye downe theire armes (theire swordes excepted): w[ch] armes, soe layed downe, shall be deliuered vp to such as Generall Mitton shall appoynt to receiue them.

Sufficient carts and teams were provided. No one was to be reproached, or have any disgraceful speeches or affront offered them. Major-General Mytton allowed Colonel Salesbury for his present subsistence so much of his own property, corn, grain and provision now in the castle as he should consider expedient 'by reason all his estate at p[r]sent is seized vpon, and employed to the vse of ye State.' All persons comprised within the articles should have a certificate to that effect.

Only one piece of ordnance is listed as being captured in the castle. Arms to the number of 200 were handed in

[177]A.&M. pp. 234-237 and Cal. S.P.D.

after the formal march from the castle—a significant number seeing that the original total of defenders was placed at 'very nigh 500 able-fighting men.' [178]

There were also in the castle many gentry and some riches, 'many barrels of meal, a great quantity of wheat, with other corn and victuals very plentiful. Some hundred weights of lead and bullets, no great quantity of powder and match, which they most wanted.' [179]

Sir William Myddelton, cousin of Sir Thomas, acted as the officer in charge of the siege under Mytton, and was nominally appointed governor of the captured castle. This was probably a gesture of courtesy as his grandfather had been governor in Elizabeth's reign. It was not long before Lieutenant-Colonel George Twisleton became military governor of Denbigh Castle, and alderman of the borough —an office he occupied for about twelve years.

More attention could now be paid to Conway which, under Sir John Owen, still defied the encircling Parliamentarians. Sir John, and his brother William who commanded Harlech, had apparently come to a mutual arrangement whereby each would hold out as long as the other. John gave way first, and on November 18, the Conway garrison marched out into the town which their adversaries had occupied for a matter of three months.

As the year drew to a close only two castles in the land flew the royal colours—little Holt beside the Dee, and far-off Harlech on its cliff top overlooking Cardigan Bay.

Before December was ended the Parliament passed an order for the 'slighting' of the castles of Flint, Rhuddlan, Ruthin, Hawarden and Holt—the latter even before it was in their hands, so sure were they of its capitulation. Stout walls which had resisted cannon fire were blown up by engineers.

✿   ✿   ✿

Holt, which stood on the river bank a short distance from the arched bridge which spans the Dee below Farndon, was in the hands of a Denbighshire worthy, Sir Richard

---

[178] *A.&M.* p. 225.
[179] *Phillips.* vol. 2. p. 329.

Lloyd, one of the irreconcilables who meant to fight to the bitter end.

'Holt hath been besieged ever since the taking of Chester', was the comment in a Parliamentary report in May. 'It is a very strong place. Starving is the only way that we can use against the place.' [180]

It had caused Mytton trouble even as early as April when he reported: 'The siege of Hoult hath of late been of great difficulty and hazard to those few men I have there, for the drawing off of the Cheshire fire-locks from that service without my privity gave the enemy an advantage to burn the guard the fire-locks kept (which cost the country much to fortify), and about forty dwelling-houses more in the town, and exposed my men (who lay in open quarters, and fewer in number than the enemy within were) to their power, which necessitated my men to be upon continual duty.'

But, despite resistence and destruction, the siege had to end and in January, 1647, Colonel John Carter, concluded the articles of surrender with Sir Richard Lloyd. On January 13, Colonel Roger Pope accepted the surrender in the absence of General Mytton.

Only Harlech remained, the last castle to hold out for the king in England and Wales. On March 15, 1647, the articles of agreement were concluded. The governor Colonel William Owen, appointed as his commissioners Sir Arthur Blayney and Captain William Edwards. General Mytton was represented by Thomas Edwardes, described as 'Adjutant-General', and Major Edward Moore. Officers and soldiers were allowed to march out with full military honours to a place within four miles and there lay down their arms. There were in the castle, Mr. John Edwards of Chirk 'who being somewhat aged died in February', in addition to his son, Captain William Edwards, Lieutenant Roger Arthur and other officers. John Edwards and his son William had previously been in Denbigh during the siege. Besides these there were twenty-eight common soldiers. Comment is made

---

[180]*Phillips.* vol. 2. p. 308.

Conway Castle.

that on March 14, 'Mr. Robert Foulkes, being in the castle, died, and was buried at Llanfair.'

The keys were delivered to General Mytton on March 16.[181]

The following tabulated list of the dates on which the castles surrendered must be regarded as an approximate guide. In some instances the date refers to the signing of the articles of surrender; in others to the actual vacation.

1646	Date	Governor
CHIRK	February 23[182]	Sir John Watts
HAWARDEN	March 16	Sir William Neale
RUTHIN	April 12	Col. Mark Trevor
ABERYSTWYTH	April 14	Col. Roger Whitley
CAERNARVON	June 4	Lord Byron
BEAUMARIS	June 14	Col. Rd. Bulkeley
RHUDDLAN	July (end)	Col. Gilbert Byron
CONWAY (town)	August 9	—
FLINT	August 24	Col. Roger Mostyn
DENBIGH	October 26	Col. Wm. Salesbury
CONWAY	November 18	Sir John Owen
1647		
HOLT	January 13	Sir Rd. Lloyd
HARLECH	March 15	Col. Wm. Owen

✿ ✿ ✿

Once hostilities ceased the victorious Parliamentarians were confronted with problems of a new order. They had to set in motion the administrative machine. Economy demanded that they should disband the armed forces as rapidly as possible yet they must retain sufficient garrisons to prevent disgruntled Cavaliers from revolting. They had to attend to the sequestration of Royalist estates. Adventurers felt the urge to feather their nests with as little delay as possible. Conscientious officers were concerned with the injurious effects of relaxed discipline.

---

[181]*Phillips.* vol. 2. pp. 332-4.
[182]William Maurice gives the date as the last day of February. Malbon states the garrison "stoole all pryvately awaye".

CONWAY CASTLE, SOUTH SIDE

This camera study by Mr. W. W. Harris of Conway, depicts the massive walls against which Mytton turned his artillery

CONWAY CASTLE AND QUAY

*Despite Telford's bridge this painting probably creates a clearer conception of seventeenth century
Conway than do most prints. It is by W. H. Bartlett (J. C. Armitage, lithographer) and was
published by George Virtue, London, in 1841*

In the summer of 1646 troopers stationed in the Vale of Conway became 'very troublesome'. Grace Wynn at Gwydir found that the country was so full of soldiers that there was no going out without danger. From Trefriw to Penmachno the country people were troubled by the lawlessness of three troops of Cheshire and Lancashire horse. Mention was made of a rifled trunk or two, and the soldiers' threats to extend their depredations as far as Dolwyddelan if their pay was not forthcoming. Some soldiers who called at Gwydir were civil, others were very rude. More soldiers departed to cross the mountains to Harlech to assist in the siege operations there.[183]

The problem of finding accommodation for mounted men was continually under discussion. Archbishop Williams considered horse 'a cruel burden' and advised Parliament to 'disband or dispose of the troops in Wales as fast as you can because of their unruliness, and to suppress all useless garrisons which will but suck out the maintenance of the army.' Mytton, having fallen ill, returned to his home at Halston whence he wrote Cromwell emphasising that Caernarvonshire was 'not a fit county to accommodate horse.' [184] Correspondence of the period abounds in such expressions as 'the insupportable burden of the free quartering of troops', or 'the insufferable burden it groans under'. In January 1648 Fairfax issued instructions for disbanding the forces in North Wales. Garrisons, however, were to be retained at Conway, Caernarvon, Beaumaris, Denbigh and Red Castle (Welshpool). Caernarvon, Denbigh and Red Castle were to retain each one gunner, two matrosses (assistant gunners) and one marshal. Gunners received 1s. 4d. per day, a marshal 10d. and a matross 4d.[185] Archbishop Williams strove to have the number of men in the garrisons reduced and succeeded in getting the quota at Conway placed at forty with fifty at Caernarvon.

In March that year came a welcome announcement. 'The inhabitants of Caernarvon have paid in their proportion

---

[183]*C.W.P.* 1802.
[184]Ibid. 1837.
[185]Ibid. 1845.

of the disbanding money and are, therefore, not to have any free quarter put upon them.'[186] The prelate doubtless thought only of sparing the purses of his countrymen; Colonel John Carter, governor of Conway, viewed the diminution of the forces with apprehension.

Following an insurrection of the inhabitants of the upper parts of Caernarvonshire, he unburdened himself to Fairfax. His troopers, he wrote, which were to quarter there had been beaten out of the counties 'in opposition and contempt of authority of your Excellency and Parliament'. When they had beaten and disarmed officers and soldiers the insurgents called them 'rebels that fought against the king.' [187]

No sooner had the Royalists driven the troops of horse out of the hinterland than they rose in the lower parts of the county 'and fell upon some of the garrison soldiers of Conway, who were sent out to assist the Constables in gathering in the contributions laid, by their own warrants, for the maintenance of the garrison.' Having wounded the officers and some of the soldiers, they took their arms away and held them prisoners. 'And all this they have done unto men quiet and civil in their quarters, that never did the country one pennyworth of harm or wrong.' [188]

In such an atmosphere resentment at the treatment accorded the king in captivity proved inflamable material.

In the spring of 1648 the smouldering embers of Royalist indignation burst into flame.

END OF THE FIRST CIVIL WAR

---

[186]Ibid. 1850.
[187]Ibid. 1811.
[188]Ibid. 1811.

CHAPTER THIRTEEN

THE SECOND CIVIL WAR

1648

IT was not until the closing stages of the first Civil War
that the tranquillity of Caernarvonshire was disturbed. In
examining the Quarter Sessions records for 1642-1645 in the
County Archives little reference to hostilities will be encountered.[189] The justices were normally occupied in dealing
with assaults, abuse, trespass, and thefts. Occasionally when
a war-note is encountered it derives from resistance to constables when they endeavoured to 'press' men for the armed
forces. A case occurred in October 1643. A justice of the
peace, Humffrey Jones of Penrhyn, heard a charge of assaulting two petty constables preferred against Thomas Lewis, a
Llandegai miller, and his two sons, David Thomas Lewis of
Pentir, and William Thomas Lewis of Vaynol. The men had
refused to accept press money and slighted the officers'
authority. When the constables were escorting them to
Penrhyn, the senior defendant threw one of the constables
to the ground, beating him and drawing blood. He called
upon his sons to beat and kill the other constable, exclaiming
that it was 'as good for them to venture their lives there as
elsewhere.' The accused were committed to prison and, after
appearing at the Quarter Sessions, were 'sent to the king's
service.' The sheriff at the time was Colonel Thomas Madryn
who, a few years later, became an outstanding Parliamentarian.

Disturbances were not invariably of this nature. The
secluded churchyard of Llannor, near Pwllheli, was the
scene of strife one Sunday morning.

Dissension arose when a recusant family (that of
Griffith Wynne of Brynhynog, gentleman, and his wife
Dorothy) were reproached for not attending the parish

---

[189]The writer is indebted to the County Archivist, Mr. W. Ogwen
Williams, M.A., for his ready assistance.

church. Upon this Dorothy expressed a wish to wash her hands in Protestants' heart's blood, and hoped that all who would not be converted to the Popish religion should have their heads 'cut off like crows' heads.' They were accompanied by several soldiers among whom were Lieutenant-Colonel Pugh and Captain William Edwards. Weapons were drawn and in the affray Captain Edwards was struck on the brow with a stone.

On another occasion when a constable was trying to impress Thomas Griffith of Llanaelhaiarn, a bystander, Harry Edwards, who went to the aid of the constable, nearly lost an eye.

Once Lord Byron established himself at Caernarvon in the spring of 1646 the county felt the rough grasp of his avaricious hand. His lordship dispatched parties of war-hardened veterans to collect money for his depleted war-chest. Robert William and David ap Robert of Llannor, demurring at having to pay in excess of their contribution, were informed that unless they did so they could 'expect noe lesse than to be plundered by a company of horsemen sent about for that purpose.'

Dame Elizabeth Bodvel, mother of the Royalist, Colonel John Bodvel, had cause to complain of a party of horse calling to collect contributions levied by Lord Byron. She had, at the time, fourteen soldiers quartered in her home, and because she could not accommodate the troopers they brought straw and threatened to burn the house and to carry her off.

It is reassuring to find an instance of a 'maimed soldiers' mize', proof that locally at all events some compassion was felt for those who suffered in the war.

✻   ✻   ✻

The Second Civil War as far as North Wales was concerned resolved itself into Sir John Owen's revolt in May, 1648, and Colonel Richard Bulkeley's uprising in Anglesey in September that year. To these might be added sundry plottings which intensified with the advent of the Restoration.

Not far from the London-to-Holyhead road near Pentre-voelas is a humble cottage with a massive porch. *Inside* this is a wall sundial on which is carved MOVNT-V-RANDEVO and the date 1648.[190] The thick walls of the house are pierced in several places by small square loopholes as if for musketry. Local tradition claims that this is the spot where Sir John's Cavaliers rallied in the momentous spring of 1648. The position of the sundial indicates it is not *in situ.*

Horse and foot to the number of a couple of hundred made their way surreptitiously to the meeting place. Most of the volunteers were officers. Messengers arrived with the enheartening news that small parties of indignant Royalists were wending their way from mid-Wales to swell the ranks.

Disquieting rumours of the unrest filtered through to the parliamentary strongholds, causing apprehension, for the garrisons were all below strength.

On May 9, sheriffs, justices of the peace, and other leading Parliamentarians held a meeting at Wrexham where it was decided to put the country 'in a posture of defence' against all who were in arms to resist the Parliament. The declaration was published in all six North Wales counties, and with it an appeal for volunteers and funds.

The sum of £6,000 was to be collected each month and the six counties pledged themselves to help each other. Persons ready to volunteer for service in Denbigh county were to send their names to Lieutenant-Colonel George Twisleton, governor of Denbigh, the High Sheriff, Sir Thomas Myddelton, or Simon Thelwall, the elder, of Plas-y-Ward, Member of Parliament and colonel of horse. The leaders in Flint were the High Sheriff, Colonel Thomas Ravenscroft, Colonel John Aldersey (these two, it will be recalled, were in charge of Hawarden Castle when it surrendered to Brereton in 1643), John Salisbury of Bachygraig, and Captain Luke Lloyd. The arms of the inhabitants in the counties of Denbigh and Flint were to be stored in Denbigh Castle. Ruthin and Rhuddlan castles were to be made 'more untenable.'[191]

---

[190]Illustration in *The Heart of Northern Wales.* vol. 2. p. 488.
[191]*Phillips.* vol. 2. p. 372.

Major-General Mytton was in Caernarvon Castle and with him the new High Sheriff, William Lloyd of Plashen (whose signature is to be seen on documents in the Archivist's office). The seriousness of the situation was impressed on the commander-in-chief when, on riding to Beaumaris, he found the gates closed in his face. Captain Thomas Symkys, who once commanded the general's own troop of horse, had gone over to the rebels!

In this time of crisis the most active officer and the one exhibiting the most initiative was undoubtedly Colonel George Twisleton, the governor of Denbigh. Assembling sixty or seventy mounted men he rode into the Snowdon fastnesses hoping to prevent the arrival of Royalists from the south and, if possible, to catch the ringleader himself.

Those who rode out with Sir John Owen included Colonel Richard Lloyd of Llwyn-y-Maen, Shropshire, Lieut.-Colonel Scriven, Colonel Lee, Morgan Herbert and Captain Edward Herbert, his son, Captain Blodwst, Captain Kynaston, Captain Phillips, Sir Arthur Blayney, Mr. Herbert Vaughan, Lieutenant-Colonel Hughes, Captain Morgan and Captain Brynkir. They were with Owen when, at the head of a hundred volunteers 'almost all of them being commanders', he rode into Dolgelley. Here they stayed two nights and, on their departure, 'paid for their quarters', explains the scribe virtuously, 'and did no man harm.' [192]

They rode to Dyffryn Ardudwy, thence into Caernarvonshire, and back to Ardudwy. This was about mid-May.

Meanwhile Colonel Twisleton and Captain Roger Sontley, having ridden from Denbigh, arrived at Dolgelley after Sir John had departed. Here they learnt that 'some foot came over Dyfy from Sir Richard Price to Sir John Owen', so they took horse for Penal and thence to Towyn. At Llwyngwril they overtook some of the footmen for whom they searched 'who, thinking they had been some of their own men, made no resistence nor shift for themselves, and therefore about forty-eight were taken prisoners, among whom

[192]*Parry.* p. 390.

were Captain Vaughan, Henry Vaughan's son of Golden Grove.'[193]

The successful Parliamentarians returned to Dolgelley by six in the evening. About midnight they took their prisoners and marched by way of Bala back to Denbigh. Meanwhile word reached Sir John Owen that his enemies were at Dolgelley so he turned back from Ardudwy but learning he had missed his quarry, he headed for Caernarvonshire.

So it was that early in June Sir John came bravely down from the hills and turned his face towards Caernarvon.

General Mytton was anxious to crush the uprising before it attained dangerous proportions and he sent to Twisleton at Denbigh instructing him to raise as large a force as possible to strengthen Caernarvon. The original orders were to advance by way of Llanrwst bridge.

Meanwhile the Parliamentary commander, learning of Owen's proximity, decided with the meagre forces at his disposal to make contact with the Royalists. To discourage any latent loyalist sentiment among people in the neighbourhood he made several sallies, the High Sheriff, William Lloyd, taking command of the horse. Colonel Thomas Madryn also assisted.

On Saturday, June 3, a small force of horse and foot were making their way along an old road which is now practicaly obliterated by the woods in Glynllifon Park. The advance guard of Owen's party appeared and there was a sharp clash. Sheriff Lloyd at the head of twenty horse bore the brunt of it, Mytton, who commanded sixty foot, being farther behind. The sheriff, wounded in some seven places, was unhorsed and taken prisoner. Mytton by a skilful movement was able to retire to Caernarvon where he found temporary security behind the stout walls. Nevertheless he dispatched a messenger post haste to Twisleton, urging him to hasten to his aid. In the meantime Twisleton had collected some seventy soldiers from Chester and, uniting these with the Denbigh garrison, he hurried to join Colonel John Carter

---

[193]Ibid. p. 390.

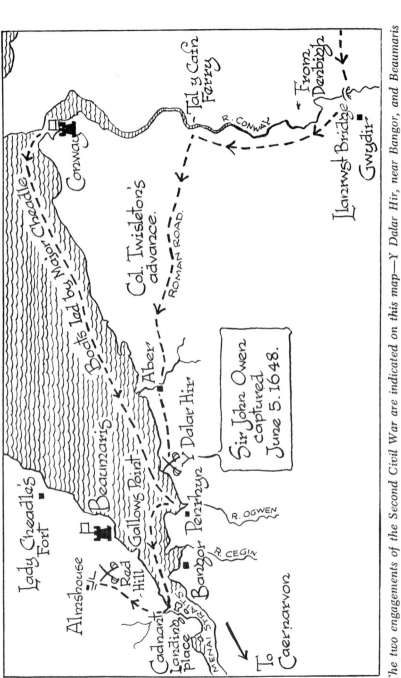

The two engagements of the Second Civil War are indicated on this map—Y Dalar Hir, near Bangor, and Beaumaris at Conway. According to Edmund Hyde Hall the force travelled by way of Bwlch-y-ddeufaen, dragging two small field-pieces with them.[194] Their intention was to reinforce Mytton in Caernarvon but it was not to be. For Owen, hearing of their approach, abandoned his vigil at Caernarvon and leaving a small party to prevent Mytton emerging, he led the remainder to intercept the advancing relief column. As his men splashed through the shallows of the Ogwen River they sighted their enemy advancing along the flat lands which border the mouth of the Menai Straits.

The entire story may be told in the words contained in 'The Narrative' which was submitted to the Parliament after the clash at Y Dalar Hir on June 5, 1648.

'Sir John Owen, Commander in chiefe of the enemies Forces (and whom they called) and formerly Major Generall against the Parliament, with a hundred and forty horse, and one hundred and twenty foot or thereabouts, was growne so strong by some addition from the Countrey, that Major Generall Mitton together with William Lloyd Esquire, High Sheriffe of Carnarven, were forced for their security to repaire to Carnarvan Garrison, upon Saturday the third instant. Major Generall Mitton with the Sheriffe and what horse were in the Garrison, being about twenty, and some Foot to the number of sixty or thereabouts, marched forth (sic) the enemy: met them within three miles of the Garrison; the Sheriffe who led the horse was so farre ingaged, that being overpowred, he could not come off, but after long strugling, having received seven or eight wounds, became their prisoner, whose barbarous usage towards him can hardly be related; they carried him, whilst he was able to sit, from place to place on horseback, his wounds never searched nor dressed, which had they been, its conceived they had not proved mortall, as by a Chirurgeons attestation appears, given by him under his hand, as followeth.

The Chirurgeons Attestation.

' "William Griffith, Chirurgeon, being sent for to dresse some men belonging to Sir John Owen, found the High

[194]*Hyde Hall.* p. 238.

Sheriffe of Carnarvan-shire, wounded in seven severall places, besides burnings and skars, but no considerable helpe afforded for the healing of them, being un-searched, untended, unrolled, from Saturday in the forenoon, untill Sunday night only some shallow pledgets of Lint on the superficies of the Orificies, which wounds (I believe) were all curable, if he might have rested in a settled place butt; being marching in wind and raine, and cold getting into the wounds must needs cause death, and this I testify under my hand.

William Griffith."

'But when his strength began to faile, they carried him upon a Beare; and all this not sufficing to take away his life, they threw him off the said beare with such violence that he presently died, having continued in the languishing condition aforesaid, from Saturday till Monday following, after his wounding; fresh cloaths being brought to him, Sir John would not suffer him to be shifted and Major General Mitton, sending to desire that he might come to Carnarvan to have his wounds dressed, with engagement that after his recovery he should render himself prisoner, it was wholly refused, and no answer returned thereunto.'

From this it will be seen that the inhumane treatment of the High Sheriff and his untimely end made a profound impression on General Mytton and his colleagues. Normally the first thought of an officer who has crushed a revolt and captured the instigator would be to report the success of his operations, but in this instance the conflict is relegated to second place. Having unburdened his mind the writer then turns to what has become known as the battle of Y Dalar Hir. So far as numbers were concerned it did not merit so imposing a designation yet the engagement resulting as it did in the capture of Sir John Owen was undoubtedly im-portant. Both sides were without distinctive uniforms and as neither side wore scarves or brassards (which is apparently what is meant by their being 'without bands') and having war-cries of a similar sound, confusion resulted. The pam-phlet continues:—

Colonel Carter Governour of Conway, and Lieutenant Colonel Twisselton, Governour of Denby used their best endeavours to suppresse the Forces raised by Sir Owen (sic) as aforesaid, and having mounted thirty foot from Denby Castle with Colonel Jones his Troop, and about thirty Volunteers mounted, being some late disbanded officers and others well-affected in Denbyshire, as also seventy Foot and thirty Horse, procured from Colonel Duckingfield, Governour of Chester, together with thirty of Colonel Carters souldiers marched towards Carnarvan, intending before ingagement with the enemy, to adde some of the Forces in Carnarvan; but the enemy prevented this, and met them upon Munday, the fifth of this instant moneth, upon a plaine near the sea-side betwixt Bangor and Aben (Aber); the Forlorns of both Parties being drawne forth, charged each other with great resolution; but ours at last were forced to a disorderly retreat; the enemy pursued with much courage, and were entertained by our reserve, after some long encounter, to their totall routing; and in their retreat Captaine Taylor singled out Sir John Owen, and after some short encounter wounded him, and unhorsing him, took him prisoner; there were of the enemy slaine about thirty, whereof three Captains, one Captaine Madrin; Captaine Morgan, and another, and fifty eight taken prisoners, most horse, whereof many of quality, as by the list appeareth; they threw away their Armes, and most of them possessed by us; few of them had escaped, but that our words were somewhat alike in sound, and the signall on both sides the same; their word was Resolution, ours Religion; the signall was without bands, so in the disorderly pursuit, we knew not each other; about fifty of their horse got away in a body, and carried three of our men with them, which we hear since they have put to death, it being according to their resolution, as some of the prisoners confest, not to give any quarter to any they took. Sir John Owen, after he was disarmed, upon discourse uttered these words; though you have defeated me, yet foure score thousand men, now in Armes in Essex and Kent will not be baffled therewith; and seemed therewith much to comfort himselfe.'

This pamphlet must be accepted as an official document as it was 'ordered by the Commons in Parliament assembled, that this Narrative, together with the Letters be forthwith Printed and Published.' Having presented his brief summary of the fight the writer reverts to the death of the High Sheriff.

'By the Barbarous, and unchristian-like usage afore-mentioned by the said Sir John Owen and his rebellious crew, towards the aforesaid Gallant Gentleman, the late High Sheriffe of Carnarvan (who with his life, gave testimony of his good affection to Parliament, Mauger[195] the late aspersions endeavoured to be fastened upon him by some persons really disaffected both to him and Parliament) as also towards others taken by them prisoners, all unbyased men and of any ingenuity and conscience, may discover their bloudy resolution, and others of their stampe towards the Parliament and their adherents. Did not God in mercy prevent the execution of their bloudy designes, as he hath been pleased most eminently of late (especially in this expedition, and that successe in Kent, and other parts of the Kingdome so manifest) which is hoped and desired, may prove as an eye-salve to open the eyes of such, as have been, or are apt to be deceived by the plausable Pretences of Malignants and Cavaliers, and serve as a motive to all honest and religious men, to lay aside divisions, and to unite against the common adversary, for the preserva-tion of Religion, and publick peace of the Kingdome.'

Mytton's letter to the Speaker in which he signs himself 'Tho: Mitton', is virtually a repetition of the facts though he mentions that when the sheriff was taken, the Royalists also captured two private soldiers. The parliamentary party secured a Royalist lieutenant and an ensign, and 'killed one of theirs.'

Mytton asserts that he personally sent three letters to Sir John Owen asking him to release Lloyd until his wounds

[195]NOTE. *Maugre*=in spite of. The treatment of Lloyd might have been prompted by personal animosity. Professor Dodd points out Lloyd had been put under arrest when war broke out as one of the trio of 'dis-affected' spirits in Caernarvonshire (*vide* Caerns. H.S. *Tr.* vol. 14, p. 26).

were healed, adding: 'I did engage my selfe that he should become a prisoner againe.'

The dispatch sent jointly to the Speaker by Colonel John Carter and Lieutenant-Colonel George Twisleton (included in the brochure) reveals the writer as something more cultured than a rough soldier. It is unlike Carter's crude style and was probably Twisleton's work.

'Honourable Sir,

The sad distempers of these times had reached these countreyes in a great Measure, and threatened sad things to these Parts, had not God been pleased to give the Enemy a blow, and such an one, as we hope will crush and destroy all their hopes in these Parts; and it is exceeding seasonable, all circumstances considered, the relation whereof we leave to this bearer, whose favour and courage, much conduced to the service; Sir John Owen hearing of our march, and suspecting our intention, which was to joyn with Generall Mytton, he as he since confessed, resolved to engage us to hinder it, and accordingly marched with all the strength he could make, which was of Reformados and Fightingmen about 250, all well appointed, and of Countreymen a numerous many, and met us between Bangor and Aber in a very faire plain upon the Sea-side; where he found us ready to entertain him, having had intelligence of his advance, we were horse and foot 200 and upwards, the dispute was desperate and hazardous, but at last (although at first our forlorn was routed) through the resolutions of the Officers and Reserves, the Routed Partie rallied, we utterly routed the Enemy, killed and tooke many; and with no few knocks to our selves; this indorsed list showes you the names and qualities of the Prisoners and their number; we dispersed also all the Clubmen that were gotten together, there is some horses of the Enemies gotten away which we could not immediately pursue, our horse being wearied in the fight and march, but intend to give them little rest in these Parts. We thought it our duty to present you with this accompt, wherein we would ascribe all to that good hand of God that fought with us and for us.

We are, Honourable Sir,

Your most humble and faithfull Servants,

JOHN MARTER[196]
GEORGE TWISLETON.

A LIST OF THE NAMES OF THE PRISONERS BOTH OFFICERS AND SOULDIERS

Sir John Owens Maj. Gener.
Mr. Richard Lloyd Colonell,
Mr. William Owens,[197]
Mr. Hugh Budurdah,
Mr. Joshua Cole,
Mr. Robert Wynn,
Mr. James Kinaston, Capt.,
Mr. Matthias Lloyd,
Mr. John Wanteon,
Mr. Thomas Lloyd, Lieu.,

Mr. Robert Wynn Lieu.,
Mr. John Mathews,
Mr. Samuel Conway,
Mr. Will. Sanders, Capt.,
Mr. Gilbert Fox, Capt.,
Mr. Arthur Stapleton Cornet,
Maurice Griffith servant to Sir John Owens.
William Hide of Cheshire,
John Harrison of London.

Richard Thomas, John Thomas, William Pym, Robert Jones, William Pirhard, William Jones, Hugh Roberts, Robert Davies, William Richard, Richard George, Owen-ap-William of Caernarvanshire.

Ralph Davenport of Lancashire.

Evan Roberts, Thomas Jones, John Davies, Hugh Greene of Denbighshire.

Robert Johns, John Hughes, William Danis (No County specified), William Calladay of Hartfortshire.

Walter Morgan of Glocestershire.

Robert Creswell, William Creswell, Walter Roe, Thomas Stockwell of Shropshire.

Christopher Elmor of Lincolnshire.

David Williams, Henry Pughe of Merionethshire,

Robert Williams of Flintshire.

David Ellis of Montgomeryshire.

Benjamin Par of Carmarthenshire.

John Morris of Cardiganshire.

John Crosse, Thomas Crosse, Jeffrey Burch, John Clark of Worcestershire.

---

[196]An obvious printer's error.
[197]Sir John's son.

Rich. Baxter of Staffordshire.
Isaac Edwards of Anglesey.
John Cadwaladr of Carmarthenshire.[198]

The diversity of districts illustrates how life was dislocated by the disturbance of war.

Another pamphlet prints 'A *Letter from Chester, of the great Victory against Major Generall Sir John Owen.*' It reads:

'Noble Sir,
        There began a new insurrection in North Wales, Sir John Owen, the Kings old Major Generall, with Colonell Floyd and others were joyned, to the number of 200 besides 200 Country-men which they had raised in those parts, and were daily increasing in Merionethshire.

Major Generall Mitton, with Mr. Lloyd High-Sheriffe of that County joyned and sent to the Committee of North-Wales to assist them with what Forces they could.

We had informations here that they were resolved to give no quarter to any that served the Parliament. And by letters from Liverpool it was said that they had discovered, that had the Cavaliers had power in their Design against that Town, they had not only killed all that have joyned with the Parliament, but to put their wives and children to the Sword.

There need not much to persuade a readinesse to joyn in the suppressing of Sir John Owen; And a messenger was dispatched to Major-Generall Mitton and the Sheriffe, to assure them of speedy supplyes, and the time and place appointed.

But before they could come up, Major General Mitton and Mr. Lloyd the Sheriffe, had ingaged with them,

---

[198] A Narrative, Together with Letters Presented by Captaine Taylor, To the Honourable House of Commons, Concerning the late successe obtained by the Parliament forces in Caernarvanshire in North Wales. against Sir John Owen, and his forces, consisting of Malignant Papists and Cavaliers. As also, Of his barbarous and unparallel'd inhumane usage towards the High Sheriffe of the said County, and others of the Parliaments party taken prisoners by him. *LONDON*, Printed for Humphrey Harward and are to be sold at his Shop at the *George* upon Ludgate-hill over against the *Bel-Salvage.* 1648.

And had a very hot fight, routed the forlorne, and did good execution.

But Reserves comming up and overpowering us, Major Generall Mitton was worsted, And the Sheriffe with some others taken.

Mr. Lloyd the Sheriffe had seven wounds, And Owen promised him upon his Honour that he should have care taken of him, for curing his wounds, yet nevertheless a guard was set upon him, and hee was carried up and down from place to place, his wounds, bleeding about the streets, and no Chirugion admitted to dresse him, and at last stript and throwne upon the ground, where he lay till he bled to death.

Collonell Carter and Collonell Twisleton with a party of Horse and Foot coming up had notice of that unhappy ingagement with the enemy before they came, and were sorry for the losse of that gallant man, yet they (after debate amongst the Officers) resolved to ingage Sir John Owen if they could.

And accordingly (marched up to them) faced each other, And their Forlornes met, and fought furiously, But Col. Carters men had the worst then.

Relief being come up from both (after another dispute) both sides were at a stand, But after some charges the Parliaments Souldiers worsted them, and brak in upon them, doing execution, which they followed so close that they put them to a totall rout, so that there is now no visible fight in the field.

I have sent you (here inclosed) a List of the particulars, and doubt not but the Parliament will proceed to execute Justice against them for murthering the High-Sheriffe of that County, doing his Office.

Chester 8 June, 1648.

A List of those particulars that were killed and taken by Colonell Carter, and Col. Twisleton in North Wales.

Taken Prisoners.

Major Generall Sir John Owen taken prisoner, and wounded with three cuts on his head by Captaine Taylor, who hath his Buffe-coate, and pulled him off his Horse.

Collonnell Floyd a notorious Cavalier, that formerly served the King.

AERIAL VIEW OF RUTHIN CASTLE

Though the 19th century building to the right dominates the scene, sufficient of the walls of the Edwardian fortress remain to indicate its general design

HOLT BRIDGE AND GATEHOUSE

From an eighteenth century estate map belonging to Mr. A. D. H. Pennant, Nantlys

10 other considerable officers.
60 Prisoners taken.
Most of the Horse.
200 Armes.
30 Slaine of the Cavaliers.
4 slaine of Col. Carters men.
Many wounded on both sides.
Good Pillage taken which they plundered from the
Country.
June 10, 1648. *Imprimatur Gilb. Mabbot.*[199]

*   *   *

With these prosaic returns ends the strange story of the encounter known as the 'battle' of Y Dalar Hir. The account would be even more interesting if all the officers mentioned could be identified. It savours of the incongruous to think of this modest meadow-land attracting the attention of the House of Parliament and setting tongues talking in far-off London. 'Hir' signifies 'long', and 'dalar' is the name applied to the turning place at the end of a furrow. An English ploughman would term it a 'headland' but to translate it thus would be misleading. Interpret the word how one may, the scene today retains its homely rustic atmosphere which holds no hint of war or politics.

The whole episode, trivial to the military mind, is not without fascination. There is something incredibly daring about Sir John's lonely rendezvous, and the manner in which his horsemen rode boldly down to pen the Parliamentary commander in his great castle at Caernarvon. In contrast is the hectic mustering of the Parliamentary horse and foot. In both forces were veterans and volunteers, men of quality and humble musketeers, shoulder to shoulder in their eagerness to settle the issue.

When men like Captain Roger Sontley or Captain Edward Taylor rode the lanes of Caernarvonshire they were far indeed from their Bromfield homes.

The alleged murder of the High Sheriff (who was akin to the Royalist Lloyds of Bodidris), and the cold-blooded

---

[199]From *N.L.W.*

shooting of the three Roundhead captives, suggest a callousness which is ill-pleasing. At the same time these incidents serve to impress on the mind something of the fierceness of the passions stirred by the plight of the imprisoned king. Charles's followers foresaw the end of their royal master unless they, by their exertions, could save him from the headsman's axe.

The valorous Captain Taylor was sent to the capital as bearer of the good tidings and was duly rewarded by a grateful Parliament with a present of £200. After strutting for this brief moment on the nation's stage, Taylor resumed a less conspicuous existence in his native haunts near Wrexham where he became a respected member of the County Committee.

The family of the sheriff who had sacrificed his life for the cause he espoused received compensation extracted from the estate of the captive Sir John Owen.

Insignificant though the clash at Y Dalar Hir appears it was not without importance. Had the scales tipped the other way the whole aspect of the uprising in North Wales might have undergone considerable change. The Anglesey Royalists would doubtless have united with Owen; Cromwell, hastening from captured Pembroke, might have been forced to turn aside, and his surprise attack on the Duke of Hamilton's invading force at Preston would have been delayed.

Today the placid pastures beside the Menai Straits are undisturbed save by grazing sheep or flocks of sea-birds. It is hard to catch an echo of discordant war-cries and the clash of arms.

146

CHAPTER FOURTEEN

THE reverse at Y Dalar Hir in no wise disheartened the Royalists in North Wales. While the energetic Captain Roger Sontley of Bron Dêg was hunting fugitives in the vicinity of Dolgelley, and General Mytton and Colonel John Jones were at Pwllheli, several dashing blades in the Vale of Clwyd began plotting to rescue Sir John Owen from Denbigh Castle where he had been incarcerated. And notwithstanding a company of Roundheads being stationed in Bangor, a party of Royalists from Anglesey crossed the Menai Straits one July evening and carried off nearly forty of the enemy whom they found near Aber. Shortly after, the Anglesey men crossed to Caernarvon and took some men and horses about Chyrmog (Clynnog?).[200]

The plotters at Denbigh were headed by several local men, among them Major John Dolben of Segrwyd, Captain Charles Chambres of Plas Chambres, a Captain Cutler, and Captain Richard Parry of Plas Llanrhaiadr, a descendant of Bishop Parry of St. Asaph. They paved the way for their exploit by bribing several of the garrison.

William Maurice in his diary makes brief reference to the incident.

> 1648.—About the end of June, Mr. Dolben and Mr. Chambers of Denbigh hadd a design to take the castle of Denbighe, they scaled it in the night, and aboute sixty men got into the ulter-ward, but they were discovered, and some of them taken; they both plundered, but escaped, as is said.

A printed account—*Denbigh Castle surprised for the King, by 60 Cavaliers &c.* supplies more detail.

> 'Noble Sir.—We finde the king's party still very active in these parts; those in Anglisey that revolted will not accept of the indempnity, but resolve to keep the island for the king. Sir John Owen is acting in Denbigh

[200]*Parry.* p. 391.

castle, where with his confederates, the castle was very neare being surprized. On Monday night last, the captaine of the guard being gone to bed, they began to act their design. And there was engaged in this business for surprize of Denbigh castle (where Sir John Owen is prisoner) a corporall and a sentinell belonging to the castle, of the parliament souldiers, who had (it seems) been wrought upon by those who carried on the design, to whom large promises were made. These men we have discovered, besides some others whom we cannot yet find out, to have been corrupted by Serjeant-major Dolton, (sic)[201] Captain Cutler, Captain Parry, Captain Charles Chambers, and some others, who were the chief actors in this plot. There was a party of the cavilliers that came that night with scaling ladders, who came privily to the walls without giving any alarm at all, the corporall and the two sentinells of guard being privy to their design and confederacy. And about some 60 of the cavalliers had scaled the walls, and had got over without any opposition at all, and were within the walls at least an hour before any alarm was given, and it was a hundred to one that we had not been all surprized and ruined, but we were miraculously delivered. The aforesaid three score cavalliers that were got over, were so near entrance into the inner ward of the castle that they had but only one horselock to break, which the corporall was ready to have assisted them in, to open one of the sally ports. It so pleased God that the captain of the guard could not sleep in his bed, but was much troubled, tho' he knew not for what, and at last he resolved to rise and to walk the rounds with his souldiers, for which purpose he did get up accordingly. When he had drawn out some souldiers to walk with him about the rounds, he went with them, untill at last he espied a party got over the walls, and scaling ladders upon the walls, whereupon the alarum was given to the castle, and the towne also by these means took the alarm. But they all yeilded themselves prisoners at mercy, only some few that had got back again over the wall. And upon remark of the business, the corporal was discovered to be going with them to

---

[201]This must mean Major Dolben.

help them to open the gate. I hope this will be a sufficient warning to them all to look well about them both in that castle and also in other parts about us.

Chester City, the 8th of July, 1648.' [202]

It is not surprising to learn that before the month was out 'Sir John Owen was sent to Windsor Castle, upon a charge of high treason and murder against him, for the business in North Wales.' [203]

The conspirators were in no wise daunted by their narrow escape for William Maurice shortly after had occasion to make another entry in his diary.

July.—In this monthe, aboute the 16th., Dolbein and Chambers with their companye came before Denbighe Castle, and, in a bravado, discharged their pistols and went away.

According to Sir Frederick Rees, the Parliamentarians who betrayed the castle were Corporal Sutton and the two sentinels Privates Williams and Ashmount. The captain of the guard was Sergeant Owen.[204]

It must have been a period of anxiety for the Parliamentarians not merely in North Wales but throughout the entire country. The uprising in South Wales, headed by the former Parliamentarian leaders, Laugharne, Rice Powell and Poyer, was sufficiently serious to warrant Cromwell's appearance in person. Fairfax was wrestling with troubles in Kent and at Colchester. From Scotland the Duke of Hamilton threatened an invasion which brought Cromwell hastening from Pembroke the moment the fortress capitulated. In all parts disgruntled Royalist officers were restless and rebellious. Anglesey was no exception. Lord Byron had been secretly plotting in Lancashire and Cheshire, but seeing greater possibilities of success in isolated Anglesey he made his way thither fondly hoping he would be hailed as the

[202]*Newcome (Denbigh)* pp. 110-113; *A.&M.* p. 241; *Parry* pp. 380-381.
[203]*Parry.* p. 384. (quoting Whitelock's *Memorials*).
[204]*The Second Civil War in Wales.* Cymmrodorion Soc. *Trans.* vol. 1930-1931, p. 28.

Field-Marshal-General he designated himself. Anglesey, prompted by his suggestion, had, that July, published a manifesto, declaring for the king. It was signed by Viscount Bulkeley who, besides being the island's outstanding personality was also colonel of a trained band.[205] The thirty-six other signatories included his young son, Colonel Richard Bulkeley, Captain Thomas Symkys, former parliamentary governor of Beaumaris Castle, Colonel John Robinson now living at his Anglesey home, Monachdy, Dr. William Griffith, Carreglwyd, Colonel John Bodvel, Richard Wynne (? of Gwydir) and other leading royalists.[206]

A council of war having been held at Llangefni it was resolved that all the islanders between the ages of 16 and sixty should subscribe to a declaration proclaiming their loyal principles. The task of drawing up this document was conferred upon two clergymen, the Rev. Michael Evans, chaplain to Lord Bulkeley, and the Rev. Robert Morgan, rector of Llanddyfan, 'who had skill enough to draw it in high swelling words and bitter language,' commented the Beaumaris schoolmaster, William Williams, who wrote an account of the momentous happenings, 'and subtletie sufficient to impose it upon a well-meaning gentry and soldiery, yet wanted discretion to pen it in that wary way, and prudent style, as the state of affairs at that time did require.' [207]

The manifesto was dated 14 July, 1648.

When word was received of the invasion from Scotland led by the Duke of Hamilton, the Anglesey Royalists thought their opportunity had come. A party crossed to Llanrwst to seize the bridgehead there. Here they were joined by Colonel Roger Whitley, the Flintshire soldier who had already lost two brothers in the service of the king. Their hopes were shattered by the devastating victory Cromwell gained at Preston, and the adventurers withdrew to Anglesey. Here they were joined by Sir Arthur Blayney, the Montgomeryshire knight. Other volunteers included Major

---

[205]*Baron Hill MSS.* 5370.
[206]*Parry.* p. 387.
[207]Ibid. p. 387. Where the Manifesto is printed in full.

John Dolben, Captain Charles Chambres, Captain Robert Hughes, Captain William Eyton, Mr. Richard Parry and others from Denbighshire; Major Hugh Pennant, of Plas Ucha, Whitford, an ancestor of the antiquarian, Mr. Thomas Griffith and Mr. Thomas Davenport from Flintshire, Captain John Morgan and others from Merionethshire.

Lieut.-Colonel Hugh Hookes,[208] doubtless of the Conway family, headed the Caernarvonshire contingent. Other newcomers were Sir Faithful Fortescue (whose defection affected the issue at Edgehill) and Samuel Singleton.[209]

Parliament, well aware of what was happening, appointed a commission of five to cope with the situation: Sir Thomas Myddelton, former major-general, his eldest son and heir, Thomas Myddelton, Major-General Thomas Mytton, Colonel Simon Thelwall, the Member of Parliament, and Colonel John Jones, Maes-y-garnedd.

About a thousand men, horse and foot, mustered at Ruthin and marched by way of Llanrwst bridge to the Conway Valley gathering volunteers on their way. At Conway the party divided, some 1,500 marching to Bangor, and the remainder going by water to the Cegin Creek. The crossing of the Menai Straits was made possible by the fleet of boats collected by Major Richard Cheadle, an enemy of the Bulkeley family.

It was stated that as soon as the 1,500 horse and foot appeared at Penmaenmawr—if it was low tide they probably marched along the shore—Royalists on Beaumaris Green showed their defiance by firing cannon and muskets, beating drums and blowing trumpets 'which the enemies took little or no notice of.' [209]

After delaying four or five days at Bangor to complete preparations the Parliamentarians were 'wafted over to Cadnant in Anglesey, about Sept. 15,[210] 1648, near the fall of night; John Wiggins, of the town of Bangor being their guide.' [209]

---

[208]In Conway church is a memorial to the wife of a Lieutenant Hugh Hookes. She died in 1632.
[209]*Parry.* p. 388.
[210]Sir Frederick Rees places the date as the end of September.

The scene as the soldiers scrambled over the seaweed-covered rocks and struggled into the dingle must have presented a nocturnal picture which was ill pleasing to Royalist eyes. Despite the brave noise and clamour on Beaumaris Green, the Royalists with one exception, did nothing to prevent the landing. Major Hugh Pennant rode up with his troop on hearing of the attempt, but by that time the musketeers were ashore. From positions behind rocks and hedges they poured in a storm of shot which caused him quickly to retire. At Porthaethwy (Menai Bridge) about a quarter of a mile distant 'a strong guard of foot under the command of two officers' had been stationed but they quitted their posts 'not without strong suspicion of treachery, for it was afterwards currently famed that one of them had received 50*l* from General Mytton, before hand, for betraying the island, and that 50*l* more were promised him after he should betray it, but never paid, as all traitors are commonly cheated by those that employ them; it being a maxim among enemies themselves, to love the treason, but hate the traitors.' [211]

The following day Mytton moved his army into position preparatory to an attack on Beaumaris. In Anglesey the command of the island forces had been given to young Colonel Richard Bulkeley, heir of Viscount Bulkeley, it being 'to the Welsh nation's honour' to be led by one of their own people and not by a stranger. When this decision was made Lord Byron in disgust withdrew to Monachdy where he was guest of Colonel Robinson until a favourable wind could carry him to the Isle of Man where the great Earl of Derby was all but 'king'.

Mytton's men marched by way of Llandegfan until they could form up with their left flank not far from the almshouses which, bearing the date 1613, still stand beside the upper road. The islanders commanded by Colonel Bulkeley with Colonel Roger Whitley as second-in-command, formed in what were known as St. Mary's Fields, in the land below Red Hill park. Their left rested on the road not far from

---

[211]*Parry.* p. 388.

Gallows Point. Colonel Bulkeley's regiment of foot was in the Harp Field. The Beaumaris Company, commanded by Captain Sanders, and other infantrymen were on Red Hill fields. 'The horse were scatteringly drawn; some in the way to the almshouses, some at Mr. R. Vaughan's house (Tros yr Afon), some in the lands of the towne and elsewhere.'

Thus the two forces waited the signal to engage. It was not until three o'clock in the afternoon of October 1 that General Mytton gave the word to advance. The account written by Schoolmaster Williams is so detailed as to imply he was present during the action which lasted for a couple of hours or more. His account reads:

'The enemy made the onset, and were stoutly repulsed by Captain Sanders and the towne's company, from the hedges in the Harp Field, but the foot in the other fields did all betake themselves to flight in disorder. Major Pennant and his troop charged the enemy, in the lane coming down from the park towards Mr. Richard Vaughan's house, and was like to take Colonel Louthian prisoner; Sir Arthur Blaney and his troop charged in the back lands, and was dangerously wounded in the arm, his elbow being shattered to pieces. Colonel Bulkeley his own troop, consisting of gentlemen, made a valiant charge upon Brickes Fields, encountering with Captain Benbow, but being over-powered by far greater numbers, were forced to retreat to the barricades near Mary Ned's house, and there another charge happened, when, on the Roundhead party, Captain Benbow and Vavasor Powell (a military preacher) were wounded, and on the cavalier side, not far from the same place, one Mr. Price,[212] vicar of Bettws Abergele, in the county of Denbigh, got his mortal wound; at the same time one Captain Lloyd, of Penhwnllys, being commanded to guard the church, he locked up his men in it, and ran himself away, taking the key in his pocket, whereupon he was called Captain Church to his dying day. These men, from the steeple and church leads, and some others from Court Mawr

---

[212]Apparently a young man fresh from Oxford. The Rev. Richard Price took office at Betws-yn-Rhos in 1644; the next vicar in 1660.

garden, played very hotly upon the enemies, and killed several especially Captain Hancock of Colonel Louthian's regiment, his Lieutenant and Ensign in the clay pits and back lanes. The islanders were so full of disorder and confusion in this fight (and indeed, it might be called an affray or scuffle rather than a fight) that they were easily routed and dispersed, Colonel Bulkeley, Colonel Whitely (*sic*) and most of the commanders retiring into the castle; but let it be understood, that a great party of the island forces being the men of Talybolion and Llison, the two remotest comotes of the island under the command of Colonel John Robinson, were not come to the place of battle this day, but in their march, about Traeth Coch, hearing of the defeat of their friends at Beaumaris, returned to their own houses. Of the enemy were killed this day about forty, and of the islanders about thirty, but near four hundred taken prisoners; and now General Mytton having routed the field, and entered the towne of Beaumaris, he sent a drum to the castle, to demand the body of Colonel Bulkeley and Colonel Whitely, which, if refused to him, he would put all the prisoners taken that day to death; upon which the two colonels surrendered themselves, to save more effusion of Christian blood, and lay prisoners at the Old Place (Henblas?) until they were ransomed. The island forces then scattered.' [213]

General Mytton is said to have made his headquarters at the Old Bull Inn. The leading Royalists submitted, and articles were signed whereby the islanders agreed to pay £7,000 within fourteen days to Colonel George Twisleton, who was appointed treasurer, the money to defray the wages of the officers and soldiers employed in the expedition. When this was done the general undertook to mediate with the parliament on their behalf.

As the articles of surrender were entered into on October 2, it was obvious that no time was lost in coming to

---

[213] *Parry.* pp. 388-389.

a settlement. Colonel Bulkeley is known to have gone 'beyond the seas' and Colonel Robinson fled to Ireland.

❁   ❁   ❁

After King Charles was beheaded, Sir John Owen, in company with the Duke of Hamilton, Earl Holland, the Earl of Norwich (Goring) and Lord Capell, stood trial. The duke, Holland and Capell lost their heads, but Sir John somehow, was reprieved. He returned to Clenennau (which had been plundered in his absence) and despite a heavy fine, he was able to spend the remainder of his days in comparative peace. The esteem in which he was held is indicated by John Taylor the Water Poet who recorded that he rode to 'a place called Climenie, where the noble Sir John Owen did, with liberal welcome, entertain me.' [214]

Rupert offered Owen a high post with the army in France but Sir John felt he could still serve his sovereign better at home. Professor Dodd points out that Owen was three times put under preventive restraint—in 1651, 1655 and 1658[215]—but he survived to see a Stuart on the throne again. Holding the post of vice-admiral of North Wales he lived until 1666. Sir John lies interred in the South Caernarvonshire church of Penmorfa (near Portmadoc). The sword which Lord Capell presented to him from the scaffold is now a cherished possession of his descendant, Lord Harlech.

Owen's old enemy, Archbishop John Williams, died at Gloddaeth Hall in 1650 and is buried at Llandegai Church at the entrance to his estate at Penrhyn near Bangor. His effigy with a ponderous Latin epitaph by his biographer, Bishop Hacket, is on the south wall of the chancel.

Colonel John Carter, the Buckinghamshire adventurer who came to North Wales in 1644, married, in 1647, Elizabeth Holland, heiress of the Kinmel estate near Abergele. He was ambitious, aspired to Parliament, and was knighted by Cromwell in 1658, but after the Lord Protector's death began to trim his sails and was able to assist in the Restora-

---

[214]*A Short Relation of a long Journey.* p. 11.
[215]Caer. Hist. Soc. *Tr.* vol. 14. p. 30.

tion and so get a second knighthood from Charles II. His colleague, Colonel George Twisleton, married the heiress of Lleuar in South Caernarvonshire and is buried in St. Beuno's Church, Clynnog Fawr.

❋   ❋   ❋

The unrest which persisted long after the suppression of the 1648 revolt was probably greater than is realized. 'Several emergencies occasioned by insurrections of the malignant party' were mentioned in 1654 by Carter when he applied for the refund of money he alleged he had expended. He claimed that he had spent the sum of £504 in victualling and repairing Conway Castle. A committee appointed to investigate reported that Carter had spent his own money.[216]

In 1655 the Parliament decreed that the castles of Conway and Caernarvon must be slighted and their garrisons transferred to Denbigh and Red Castle.[217] For some reason these two splendid piles were spared the fate of the neighbouring fortresses but, whatever the reason, it is certain it would not be sentiment.

The extent of the unrest has not been brought to light but sundry references indicate that a number of Royalists stubbornly persisted in their intrigues against the unwelcome government.

Though Colonel John Robinson had been forced to flee from his Anglesey home, Mynachdy, he renewed his opposition immediately he was safely at Dublin, and in 1649 Major-General Mytton learned that Ormonde had given Robinson a commission to seize the island of Bardsey. Mytton frustrated this by dispatching Ensign Aspinall with thirty men to the island. Three days after their arrival at Bardsey they were able to seize 'Colonel Gerrard, Mr. Conwy, and six gentlemen more who landed there to surprise the island, took their boat and sent them prisoners to Caernarvon.' The report adds that the pirate who set them ashore and was an Irishman 'fled away.'[218]

---

[216]*Cal. S.P.D.* 1654. p. 18.
[217]Ibid, 1655. p. 232.
[218]*Parry.* p. 385.

There was a wide-spread conspiracy in 1655 but the few Caernarvonshire names involved in it were, writes Professor Dodd, 'mainly obscure ones'.[219] This, of course, excludes Sir John Owen who was one of those arrested. Some light is thrown on this abortive uprising in Caernarvonshire by several letters exchanged between the governor of Conway, Colonel John Carter, who was at the time visiting Cromwell in London, and his deputy, Lieutenant Thomas Kynaston whom he left in charge of Conway Castle. The originals are at the University College of North Wales. The first letter from Carter, written in March 1655, was in reply to a report from Kynaston to Cromwell informing him of a conspiracy detected near Conway, the leader of which was one Bayly, possibly of the Anglesey family of that name.

When John Taylor visited Conway in 1652 he wrote: 'I lodged at the house of one Mr. Spencer (an English man) he is post-master there.' [220] Spencer had been an officer in the Parliamentary army of invasion and it was his astuteness which uncovered the plot.

Kynaston had been warned by General 'Lord' Lambert to be on his guard and, writing to the Lord Protector, he assured him that he had shown 'double diligence'. He informed Cromwell that Ensign Spencer, formerly an ensign to Colonel Carter, and at this time post-master of Conway, 'by discoursing with a neighbouring inhabitant discovered something relating to the listing of some men designed for the putting of the bloody plot against the present Government into execution.'

William Stodart, a Justice of the Peace, examined suspected persons and took depositions. Kynaston wrote that the names were 'now enclosed' but there is no sign of them.

Edward Williams, one of the prisoners examined, was sent to the common gaol 'as conceived guilty of high treason'. Two others had entered into recognizances for their appearance when required.

[219]Caer. H.S. *Tr.* vol. 14. p. 31.
[220]*A Short Relation of a Long Journey.* p. 8.

'Mr. Bayly,' lamented Kynaston, 'the man mentioned in the examinations, is returned home amongst his neighbours.' Kynaston added that as Bayly had been so far engaged in this 'inhuman action' he could not understand how the man had been so soon cleared.[221] Colonel Carter's reply is given in full.

'For Leftennant Tho Kinnaston
     at Conway Castle,
        Co Carnarvon sheere.
These With trust and speede.
Lett^{tt} Kinnaston,
     His Hieness the Lord Protector received y^{re} letter and the Examinations of the persons suspected to bee ingaged with Bayly in the Plott and hee comanded mee to write unto you to continue y^{or} care in enqui'ring out the rest of theare complacies for certainly theare are many yet undiscouered that were ingaged with them. The examinats say that Evan Jefferise tould John Evans that hee heard Wm. Wms., Ed. Wms. and diuers others in Isaph had promised to apeere in Armes under Bayly at an howers warning.
     Its thought fitt that you send for that Evan Jefferise into Custodie and find owt the bottome of those mens ingadgm't (engagement) to Bayly; lett Jefferise proue how they became ingaged to Bayly as hee saith hee heard they weare. Else keepe him in ye Castle till you heare further and if hee doe prooue it against y^{m} or any of them or others send souldiers and fetch them into ye Castle and theare keepe them safe till further Order and send mee word with speede what you doe hearein, and examine strictly what proofe can be made of Bayliss ingaging any &.
     upon my receipt of it you shall receiue further Orders touching him also. Send also for Mr. Tho Williams of Llanbaglans man who Jefferise said was twice desired by Bayly to beare armes under him and let him be carefully examined to prooue that Bayly soe attempted him as Jefferise saith. You are desir'd to bee

[221]*The Family Papers of Owen and Stanley of Penrhos, Holyhead.* U.C.N.W. (1951). v. No. 212. I am indebted to the Librarian, Mr. Emyr Gwynne Jones, M.A., for calling attention to this correspondence.

uerry carefull of ye Castle with ye few men you haue
to preuent any surprise, and to yse all yo^{re} indeavours
to find out ye truth of these things and to . . . them up
with all the speede you can send.

                    Y^{re} uerry loving friend,
March the 5th.   Jn Carter.
1654.
Y^{re} coppise I also
receiued safe.'

'For Liften^t Kinnaston
          at Conway Castle in Carnarvon sheere.
Sir, Y^{res} I received and am comanded to tell you that
y^{re} care in this business is verry well aprooued of. I
know you will continew it. If you doe heare of any that
weare out in ye insurrection or knowing of it weare in
redyness to joyne send for them in. It may be Mr.
Madrin (to whom I have wrote) will giue you notice of
some such. Thean will bee a speedy coorse taken for to
safe you in the case of such as you haue in custodie and
weare really in ye plott. You did not send mee ye names
of all such as you haue secured. If any are secured up^o
suspition only and y^t noe proofe is against y^m of theare
beeing of ye plott such you may release taking good
security for theare quiet liuing for ye future and for
aparance on notice left at theare houses. As for ye
victualling of Conway & better manning it some speedy
course will bee directed what shall be don with that
and all other Garisons in Wales. In ye meane while I
know you will bee as careful of it as you can with ye
men you haue. I hope this storme is blowne over every
wheare.
          in hast I rem
                    Y^{re} asshured frind,
                                        Jn Carter.[222]
the 21st March. 1654.

Roger Mostyn's brief incarceration in Conway Castle in
May 1658 suggests that he was involved in some plot but
nothing seems to have come to light beyond Whitelocke's

-----

[222]*Penrhos MSS* v. 32a & 32d. U.C.N.W. (Punctuation added).

two references to his obtaining Roger's release on parole two days after his arrest.

❋　　　　❋　　　　❋

Once death removed the firm hand of Oliver from the helm of the ship of state, hopes of the Royalists soared. Unrest intensified. Confusion in Westminster and disorganisation in the army lifted high the aspirations of all who prayed for the restoration of a Stuart. Action in this area centred on the former ardent Parliamentarian, Sir George Booth, the Cheshire baronet. It was the veteran warrior Sir Thomas Myddelton of Chirk Castle who sparked the political powder in North Wales. Despite his eighty years he brandished his sword in Wrexham market-place and proclaimed Charles as king. Sir George Booth and the Earl of Derby combined to swell the throng of jubilant loyalists. To Myddelton flocked Royalist neighbours, Sir Edward Broughton of Marchwiel, Captain John Edwards of Chirkland, Colonel John Dolben of Segrwyd near Denbigh, Captain Richard Dutton of Keven-y-Wern, Captain Charles Chambers of Plas Chambers and others of Sir Thomas's erstwhile opponents. Age deprived Sir Thomas of leadership but his cloak fell upon the shoulders of his heir, another Thomas.

These men marched to Chirk Castle, began to fortify the stronghold, and awaited the storm which would inevitably break.

Sir George Booth gathered four thousand enthusiasts about him, never doubting the rest of the land would follow suit. News of the outbreak stung London into activity. The Parliament's best general, 'Lord' Lambert, set off at the head of five thousand Parliamentary soldiers intent on extinguishing the fire of revolt before it spread. Booth took Chester without a shot being fired. Liverpool and smaller places were quickly in the hands of the Royalists. Warrington was chosen as their headquarters. When it was learnt that Lambert was approaching by forced marches Booth endeavoured to negotiate but Lambert believed in the 'root and branch' policy of Cromwell. With a curt negative rejoinder he prepared to attack. His Roundheads swept down

upon the Royalists at Winnington Bridge and an utter rout
was only prevented by Captain Edward Morgan of Golden
Grove sacrificing his life to enable the residue of Booth's
forces to escape.

In a week Liverpool and the other towns which declared for Charles were in Parliamentary hands again.
Lambert marched on Chirk Castle which he proceeded to
bombard. A mortar was placed on a nearby knoll. There was
no water supply in the castle. Quickly Chirk capitulated
and the aged Sir Thomas saw his palatial home once again
in alien hands. He, himself, was declared traitor and his
estates sequestrated.

Young Captain Richard Wynn of Gwydir was caught
up in the uprising though the part he played is uncertain.
It was sufficient to land him in Caernarvon Castle where the
turncoat tyrant, Colonel Thomas Madryn, former sheriff, was
governor. The rounding up of the conspirators is briefly but
vividly sketched in a few letters among the *Wynn Papers*.
Robert Price of Gilar (probably the same Robert Price of
nearby 'Place Yollin', who compounded in 1649 for delinquency in arms)[223] wrote to his neighbour, Lady Grace
Wynn, warning her that Parliamentary troopers were search-
ing for her son.

'Madam,
  John Evans, the trumpeter, and another trooper
was here yesterday being sent purposely by Captaine
Sontley: to sumon and require my neighbour Mr.
Ellice Price; my sonne; and others to appear: and submitt themselves unto Cap. Sontley; he gives them a
weeke's tyme to come in; and to bring in their horses
and Armes; promising to use them Civilly; and to show
them all fav'r that shall lye in his power in the future
if they submit [themselves?][224] and come in to him. I
understand by the troopers and by another friend that
came yesterday from Wrexham that severall gentlemen as namely: a sonne of Mr. Salusbury of Boch
Egraig: Mr. Puliston of Emrull, Cap: Chambers &
others have submitted already, and that they are civilly

<hr />

[223]*Cal. Committee for Compounding.* vol. 3. p. 1890. Price was not fined!
[224]Damaged.

treated; I hope to understand more of their p'sedings at Bromfield ere longe. The two men that were here did onely enquire where Mr. Richard Wynne was, and I answered them the truth: that I did not know where he was but I did believe that he was not at or neer home. Sr George Booth for certain was taken at Newport Pannell: Noe other for certaine newes all being quiett in Yorkshire and all other places, as they say.

I shall trouble yr Ladyship no further; but onely subscribe that I am really, Madam,

Yr humble & faithfull servant,

ROBERT PRICE.

Geeler, 4th Sepem, 1659.

Lt. Col. Ed. Broughton is sent prisoner to Chester; it is feared that he shall lose his life upon account of having broken a former Paroll.' [225]

Price's next letter (on September 14) advised Lady Wynn that 'Col. Madryn must be made their friend if her son's estate is to be saved from the sequestrators.' Mr. Ellice Price was back from Wrexham having made his peace with the authorities. His excuse was that he had only called to see Myddelton on business. What Lady Wynn had to do must be done quickly. 'Colonel Madryn expects to be courted, and, if it be handsomely done, he may soon be gained.' [226]

Lady Wynn 'courted' successfully. The bribe must have been substantial, for on September 30 young Richard was back at his home, Caermelwr, Llanrwst, with a pass. The 'courting' was periodically resumed until Charles was on the throne. Sir Richard that same year (1660), became the fourth baronet on the death of his father. He was made chamberlain to Queen Catherine, and is said to have presented a large Conway pearl for inclusion in the new regalia which replaced the one lost in the wars.

Captain Roger Sontley who was so active a member of the Parliamentary County Committee, exhibited such zeal that he found himself ere long in a Royalist prison. The tables were reversed. In 1665 Sontley, still in Denbigh

---

[225]National Library of Wales. *Wynn (of Gwydir) Papers.* No. 2193.
[226]*C.W.P.* 2195.

Castle, wrote to Sir Richard begging him to secure him his liberty.[227]

Sir Thomas Myddelton was not long denied his home. A rebuilt wall at Chirk shows how the place was 'slighted', though not entirely wrecked. The Restoration was at hand. Sir Thomas received £60,000, to recompense him for his losses. His son was made a baronet.

A number of North Wales Royalists were nominated Knights of the Royal Oak. The knighthood never materialized for it was feared such recognition might have reopened wounds the nation desired to heal. Such nominations would have been conferred only upon men who rendered exceptionally distinguished service. The fact that some recipients are now hard to identify is an indicaton of the way in which records have been lost.

Colonel Roger Mostyn was rewarded by Charles the Second with a knighthood, quickly followed by a baronetcy. Colonel Roger Whitley became Receiver General. He entered Parliament, turned Whig, entertained William III, and served as mayor of Chester.

Major Francis Manley, thanks to his brother John, obtained a post under the Commonwealth, turned Royalist at the Restoration, and rose in the legal profession to gain a judgeship and a knighthood. Colonel Hugh Wynne con-

---

The following list of those nominated Knights of the Royal Oak is extracted from Parry's *Royal Visits and Progresses*.
ANGLESEY: John Robinson Esq., William Bould Esq., Thomas Wood Esq., — Bodden Esq., Pierce Lloyd Esq.
CAERNARVONSHIRE: Sir John Owen's heire.
DENBIGHSHIRE: Charles Salisburie Esq., Euball Thelwall Esq., Foulke Middleton Esq., John Wynne Esq., Sir Thomas Middleton, Knt. (of Chirk Castle, of Westminster after, spent most of his estate), Bevis Lloyd Esq., John Lloyd Esq.
FLINTSHIRE: Sir Roger Mostyn, Knt. of Mostyn, Bart., Sir Edward Mostyn, Knt., John Salisbury, of Bachegrag, Esq., Robert Davies Esq., John Puliston Esq., John Hanmer, Knt., Bart., William Hanmer, Esq.
MERIONETHSHIRE: William Salisbury Esq., William Price, Esq., William Vaughan Esq., Howell Vaughan Esq., — Anwyl, of Parke, Esq., Lewis Owen Esq., John Lloyd Esq.
MONTGOMERYSHIRE: John Pugh Esq., — Owen Esq., of Ruserton, — Blaney Esq., Roger Lloyd Esq., Richard Owen Esq., Richard Herbert Esq., Sir Edward Lloyd, Edmund Wareinge Esq.
[227]Ibid. 2446.

tinued to take an interest in the Caernarvonshire military affairs and served as a Deputy Lieutenant. Colonel Roger Mostyn and Colonel William Price continued to place their military experience at the disposal of the country by serving in command of the local militia. Mention is made of their companies in the *Progress* of the Duke of Beaufort through North Wales in 1685, by which time these erstwhile dashing Cavaliers had become revered veterans. 'Old Bluestockings', weakened by the memorable siege, appears to have died about the time the King returned from his wanderings. The honours which would have been bestowed upon him went to his loyal second son, Charles, who served with the colonel during the siege of Denbigh.

Exiles flocked back from the Continent. Colonel Robinson of Gwersyllt found his home restored 'by some alien hand'—presumably that of the above mentioned Roger Sontley.

The men who had sacrificed and suffered for their king might now sheathe their swords.

An old line drawing of Ruthin Castle in the British Museum

164

A FINAL WORD

W HEN the fighting ended the time came for counting the cost. In Caernarvon, for instance, the inhabitants were taxed for supporting the garrison in Caernarvon castle—taxed until complaints of overcharging were made to the justices. The Parliamentarians put down Sunday fairs, suppressed ale-houses, endeavoured to stop Sunday travelling, and even penalised a poor woman who carried a basket of nuts on Sunday.

The quay of Caernarvon town, the shire hall, and the church of Llanbeblig were 'said to be ruinous and in great decay' according to a presentment made to the grand jury in January 1648/9.

While local hunters were far afield stalking human foes on the field of battle the wild life of the county flourished unchecked to such an extent that the justices offered boun-ties for the slaughtering of foxes, polecats, hedgehogs, wild cats, stoats, otters, weasels, and two creatures by the peculiar names of 'fitchewe' and 'fayrebade'. These were evidently of small size for the bounty was only 8d. as for stoats and weasels, whereas 10/- was offered for a fox, and 2/- for an otter. Ravens figured on the condemned list, and crows were listed at 6d. a dozen.[228]

The appearance of the war-wracked country is implied in words written by John Taylor, the Water Poet, who rode this way on his nag, 'Dun' in the summer of 1652. Flint Castle he noticed was almost buried in ruin. As for the town there was 'no saddler, taylor, weaver, brewer, baker, botcher or button-maker.' He laments 'They have not so much as the signe of an alehouse, so I was doubtful of a lodging.' There was little to be seen in Rhuddlan beyond 'a wind and war-shaken castle.'

Of Conway he wrote: 'There is a good defensive castle which I would have seen, but because there was a garrison I was loath to give occasion of offence or be much in-quisitive.'

---

[228]The Caernarvonshire County Archives.

Undoubtedly he was wise—Colonel John Carter was the governor! Caernarvon impressed him as invincible. His five hours' inspection produced an unexpected sequel.

'When I thought I had taken my leave for ever of it, then was I merely deceived; for when I was a mile on my way, a trooper came galloping after me, and enforced me back to be examined by Colonel Thomas Mason (the governor there) who after a few words, when he heard my name, and knew my occasions, he used me so respectfully and bountifully, that (at his charge) I stayed all night, and by the means of him, and one Mr. Lloyd (a Justice of the Peace there) I was furnished with a guide, and something else to bear charges for one week's travel; for which courtesies, if I were not thankful, I were worth the hanging for being ungrateful.' [229]

Though the warriors of the king had laid down their arms they were by no means broken in spirit. In the Caernarvonshire archives is a presentment of a grand jury in 1648 who, despite parliamentary occupation, boldly protested against the killing at Llandegai of their 'neighbour and fellow subject', Robert ap William ap Robert of Llanllechid by Captain Oakes and his company.

'We also conceive that ye Troopes of horse commanded by Capt. Yong and Capt. Viner a charge upon the said County to be (blessed be God) uselesse amongst us and consequently an unnecessary charge.'

A warrant was issued to the sheriff and constables to demand a ten shilling fine from Thomas Glynne of Plas Newydd, esquire, for using the name of Christ in vain.

The calendar of prisoners in 1651 shows that William Jones, gentleman, was in the county gaol for uttering contempt of the present government.

In the ale-houses a similar spirit of resentment was exhibited. A former Royalist soldier, one Lewis Morris of Llanddinolen, was prosecuted for abusing the government. He was in an ale-house when a Parliamentary soldier named Robert Vaughan, who served in the Caernarvon garrison,

[229]*A Short Relation of a Long Journey.* p. 8.

entered with a sword at his side. Morris taunted him, asserted that he had been a Cavalier, and added: 'a turde in the States' teeth and I care not if they and all Roundheads were hanged.' [230]

Constables were appointed to keep watch and ward on Sundays to report and charge any persons found breaking the Sabbath. Such was Caernarvonshire under the unpopular puritan regime.

Captain William Oakes the Parliamentarian who called forth this protest from the Caernarvonshire jury following his slaying of a man at Llandegai, turned his coat before the Restoration. In September 1660 he wrote, on behalf of Sir John Carter, to Lieutenant Thomas Kynaston who had been transferred from Conway to Beaumaris. Addressing him as 'Honest Godson', Oakes stated that it was Sir John's command that Kynaston slept in Beaumaris Castle every night and that he be 'vigilantly careful of the same for his Majesty's service.' No person whatsoever under any pretence was to come into the castle without first having order from the governor, Sir John Carter.[231]

Disappointment must necessarily be felt at the paucity of information to be extracted from church registers of this period yet the very omissions are indicative of the upheaval of the times. Conway Church registers—which somehow survived—throw no light on the war scene. After 1641 a large portion of a leaf has been cut away, and entries were not resumed until 1644. In that year there were 14 deaths and 15 baptisms; in 1645 six deaths and 11 baptisms—none, apparently, directly attributable to the war. The year when Conway was under siege—1646—when the entry of deaths would have held particular significance, contained only one entry, that of a baptism. A few more baptisms occur until 1650 and then 'from here great irregularities and omission until 1699.' [232]

Of possible interest is a monumental inscription on the north side of the chancel. It is to Rowland Pugh of Math-

[230]Notes by the County Archivist, Mr. W. Ogwen Williams.
[231]Penrhos Papers, v. p. 301.
[232]The Registers of Conway. 1541-1793. Alice Hadley (1900). p. 138.

avarne, in the county of Montgomery, esquire, who died on St. Stephen's Day, 1644. It is difficult to account for his presence in Conway unless there was some association with the war.

Miss Hadley writes: 'The income of the vicar, Hugo Jones, appointed in 1642, was sequestrated in 1650.' [233]

The new system introduced during the Commonwealth is indicated by entries (upside down) made in 1655 and 1656 by 'Capten John Arundell, register.' One marriage entry for 1657 has been inserted after 1778.

Arundell turned Royalist. Sir John Carter addressed a letter to him in Conway on January 29, 1661, desiring him to inform Kynaston at Beaumaris that he was to disband all Lord Bulkeley's soldiers 'without a penny of money.' [234]

✿ ✿ ✿

To trace all the North Wales Royalists who participated in the Civil War is a hopeless task. Unless persons are specifically mentioned in the articles of surrender it is difficult to learn the identity of those who fought tenaciously for the king. Though the *Calendar of the Committee for Compounding* assists it does not always elucidate. Names which might be expected to appear are missing. Under the Denbigh articles, Thomas Whitley of Aston compounded and was fined £125 for 'deserting his habitation and going into the garrison held against parliament' but there is no mention of his son, Colonel Roger Whitley, governor of Aberystwyth. No explanation is offered for the presence in Conway Castle of Sir Thomas Eyton of Eyton (Salop) who compounded under the Conway articles and was fined £818 (altered to £976). Some names signify little. It is difficult to identify John Williams of Llanywith (Llannefydd) who was under age when he fought through the siege of Denbigh but was fined £66.

Henry Taylor published a list of 13 Flintshire 'knights and gentlemen' who compounded for their estates. Somehow the names of Colonel William Salesbury of Bachymbyd and

---

[233] Ibid. Intro. xv.
[234] *Penrhos Papers.* v. p. 20. No. 32c.

Rûg, the governor of Denbigh, and his loyal son, Charles, have intruded into the Flintshire roll. They were fined £781. Admitting they had both borne arms, Charles begged to compound for his father and himself explaining 'his father was too infirm to travel.'

The names Taylor extracted from 'the printed general catalogue of sufferers' does not invariably correspond with the *Calendar of the Committee for Compounding*. For example, the *Calendar* records Thomas Pennant's ancestor, Robert Pennant of Downing, as being fined £40.6.8 'for delinquency in taking up arms for the king'. In Taylor's list the fine is £298, and David Pennant of 'Bighton', gent. is given as paying £42.14 compared with the *Calendar's* £197 'on Denbigh articles for delinquency in arms.' Thomas Pennant in his *History of the Parishes of Whiteford and Holywell* states that the Bychton estate paid only £42.14 in the general composition but Robert Pennant of Downing was fined no less than £298—presumably because some young man in the house at Downing fired on a parliamentary detachment and wounded a cornet.

The six months' siege of Denbigh attracted so much attention that the names of any of the heroic defenders are acceptable. Those who compounded under the Denbigh articles and were fined for delinquency in arms included: Colonel John Thelwall, Plas Coch (£117), Robert Parry, Llewenny (£28), Colonel Thomas Davies, Gwysaney (£51), Edward Goodman, Nantglyn (£46.10.8), Captain John Edwards, Chirk (£80), John Eyton (senior) of Leeswood £172.15), and his son, John Eyton, junior (£42), Colonel Peter Griffiths, Caerwys (£113.13.6), John Jones (senior), Halkin (£156.11.4), Edward Lloyd, Hersketh, Mold (£64.10), and his son Thomas who petitioned that his estate should be sequestered to meet his father's delinquency fine as Edward Lloyd died shortly after the surrender. Gabriel Roberts, Segrwyd, was not fined. Major John Dolben was fined £107.

Richard Dutton of Keven-y-Werne, co. Denbigh, was fined £185.6.8 for his delinquency which was 'going to Oxford and adhering to the forces raised against the parliament.'

Robert Price, Plas Iolyn, admitted being engaged in the late wars against the Parliament, but was not fined.

Sir William Gerard, a prominent Lancashire Catholic, was among the prisoners taken at Denbigh.

Colonel Richard Lloyd, Llwyn-y-Maen, Shropshire, captured at Y Dalar Hir, who fought in both wars, was fined £480.

Colonel John Bodvel of Bodvel, Caernarvonshire, a former Member of Parliament who turned Royalist and served in Anglesey, had his affairs in so complicated a condition that the *Calendar* devotes several pages to an attempted elucidation during which it states that since his articles 'Bodville has been in the company with Charles Stuart, the late pretended King of the Scots' in Holland and elsewhere.

Taylor's list includes: Robert Davies, Gwysaney (£645.11.4), William Hanmer of Fenhall (£1,370), Edward Phillips of Worthenburg (£24), and Roger Mostyn 'of Mostin, Esq.' (£825).[235]

The *Calendar* describes Colonel Roger Mostyn as late governor of Flint Castle. He compounded for delinquency under the Flint articles but begged further time to pay his fine as 'through the opposition of Holt Castle, where many of his writings are, he cannot perfect his particular.' The time limited by the articles had nearly expired. Five weeks 'delay' was granted.

Major Francis Manley, Erbistock, was another admitted under the Denbigh articles and was fined £75. Thomas Hanmer of Apley Castle, Salop, was admitted to composition but on January 28, 1645/6, was still 'a prisoner at Wem.'

Captain Valet, the heroic governor of Beeston, was present during the siege. Malbon writes: 'The said vallatt wth his Soldiers havinge a Convaye wth theim was broughte vnto Denbighe, whether hee had a desyre to goe'.[236]

❖ ❖ ❖

At the Restoration the humble warriors who had

---

[235]*Cal. of Com. for Comp.* p. 143.
[236]*Hall.* p. 181.

suffered for their king were not wholly forgotten. In January 1661 Caernarvonshire Justices ordered Major William Spicer (who had assisted in the defence of Caernarvon Castle), with Alderman William Thomas of Caernarvon and William Robins, gentleman, to call maimed soldiers before them to ascertain if they were worthy of relief. The thirty-seven names submitted on one list include a Captain Richard Vaughan. The detailed list speaks so eloquently that it is printed without comment.

Roland ap Robert Edmund, an adged man of 63 yeares, hath been served in Scotland and other places under Sr John Owen, hath a slender wound on the knee.

Robert Owen of Caerhun, maymed of the hand and wounded on the head in Nasbie fight, a very poor man.

John Griffith ap Hughe of Langwnadle, wounded in several places upon several parts of his body.

Roland Hughes of Caerhun, wounded in the head, necke and shoulder.

John Williams of Pethkelert, in Nasby fight hurt in the legge and the thighe, a great wound.

Thomas ap Richard Owen of Nevyn, wounded on the shoulder.

Edward Griffith of Bryncroes, wounded on the head.

Roland Owen of Clynog, hurt and made a criple.

Hugh Owen of Aberdaron, shott and cut in two places, namely on the shoulder and arms.

David Owen of Conway, shott under the eye very dangerously and the bullet remained under the ear, and have several wounds.

William Morris of Llanarmon, quite maymed and half lost his right hand being shott with a Canon bullett.

John Owen of Llanyestyn, wounded in the thigh and hurt and have lost the use of his left hand being maymed of itt.

Symon Davies of Castell, wounded in divers places as in the thigh, side and his head.

Hugh James of Llanvihangel, an old soldier greatly wounded and have served under several commanders.

William Lloyd of Llanvairisgaer, hurt and wounded in divers parts of his bodie.

Edward Ellis of Carnarvon, hurt and wounded on the shoulder and have lost ye use of his arme under Capt. Brynkir.

William ap Richard of Llanbeblig, shott at Whitchurch in the right arm, and have lost the use of.

William Griffith of Llanllechid, aged 87, an old soldier to Queen Elizabeth, King James and the late king, hath several wounds and lost two sons in the King's service and is most considerable (i.e. worthy of consideration).

John Ellis of Llanbeblig was shott in the legge a slight wound.

Robert Evans of Bangor lost his left hand and hath other wounds received on the King's service.

David Thomas of Llanllechid shot and hurt in several places of the body, very sore hurt and the skull crackt.

Rytherch ap Edward of Llysfaen, aged 76 years, have served in Queen Elizabeth's time and in the King's service and have several wounds received in their service and deserveth consideration.

Symon ap William Lewis of Llanbeblig, shott under the eare and out at the chop, and also in the shoulder whereof he still languiseth.

Evan ap Ellis of Llandden' has several wounds and cuts, a very poor man.

Harry ap Rees of Llanllechid, aged 72 years, has lost the use of both hands in the King's service.

Humphrey John William of Pwlheli has lost ye use of his left Arm and is a very poor man and deeply hurt.

William Roberts of Carnarvon hath been shot in the foot and wounded in the head.

Maurice Hughes of Ynyskynhaynon, an ancient man, and shott in ye knee and thereby lost the use of one side and a very poor man.

Jane verch Hugh of Carnarvon, a poore widow of 80 years of age whose husband was a Taylor and was killed in Ireland under my lo. of Ormonde in ye late King's service by reason whereof she is deprived of her livelihood and is in great poverty and deserveth to be considered.

Edmund Wynne, late soldier to his Mat.^{e} Charles the first in severall parts of England and Wales, hath had severall shott in his body during the said warre to his great detriment.

David Lloyd, late of Llysfaen, was a soldier to his Majestie Charles the first in several parts of England, shott in the knee.[237]

John ap John Lewis of Rhug, aged 74 years, an old soldier and have great and many wounds on several parts of his body.

Elsewhere there is a record of a petition to the Caernarvon magistrates[238] : —

> 'John ap John Lewis, have done service in warre for his countrie for the space of nine yeares at Ireland and Scotland, and now beeing poore and aged and not haveing wherewithall to maintaine himself desireth that y^r worships be pleased to comisserat his distress'd case & to allow him some maintenance & reliefe out of the maimed-souldiers mise as formerly ye pet^r (petitioner) was wont to have.'

There is a natural tendency to regard the wars of the past from the viewpoint of officers. Perhaps this is inevitable as this is the source from which information usually springs. It is, therefore, not unseemly, that this record of the struggle should conclude with these references to the humble warriors whose faithful service made great issues possible but whose names remain unrecorded in the annals of the race.

END

---

[237]Caernarvonshire County Archives. I am indebted to Mr. W. Ogwen Williams, M.A., County Archivist, for his kind assistance in obtaining this information.
[238]Caernarvonshire County Archives, 1655 file.

APPENDIX A

PREPARATIONS BY THE ANGLESEY COMMISSION
OF ARRAY

January 27mo. Proposicoñs to bee considered of by the
Comee of Arraye and peace for the County of Anglesey.

1, THAT in this time of imminent danger wherein wee
are now threatened wth an invasion from seuall pts there be
some speedy course resolved on, and seriously putt in ex-
ecuccoñ for the defence of the Island wch is to be done by
frequent musteringe and trayneinge the whole fourses of the
County requiring all men w'soever by their bodies or purses
or both to endeav'r the safety & preservation of themselves
& their Countrey and that under such a penalty to be in-
flicted upon defaulters as shall be able to p'cure or enforce
obedience.

2, By levyinge of moneys for the p'urement of Ammunition & fire armes.

3, By fortifying the maritime partes and landing
places of the Island.

4, By supplyinge the seuall Garrisons of Beaumaris
and Holyhead wth necessary provision for six months at
least and by causing the monthly contribucoñs to be duely
paid in for the support and the encouragement of the
Soldiers in each Garrison and by punishinge such as are
refractory therein.

5, By takeinge some p'indent and discreet course for
the Disapointment of practices against the peace and wel-
fare of this Country if uppon due examinatoñ any such
appear to bee, or be probably suspected.

U.C.N.W. Baron Hill MSS, 5363.

APPENDIX B

BEAUMARIS BEEF FOR CAPTAIN BALDWIN WAKE

To our Very Loveinge Ffriend Mr. Michael Lewes, These. in Bewmares.

Mr. Michael Lewes. There being a present necessity of vittualing Captaine Wake, and the other Shippes now with him in Chester watter, and, understandinge that you have 80—or 100 Barrells of Beefe ready salted and fitt ffor Shippinge at Bewmarys wee have thought to make lese of 16,000 weight of the Beefe ffor him and wee doe undertake to satisfie you fforthw^th Accordinge to such rates, as shalbe reasonably Agreed on by Capt. Chedle and your Selfe, no Corne or other provisions of vittualls, and this beinge ffor the present use of the ffleett wee make noe doubt that you will readily Comply w'th our order and desire herein, Soe wee bidd you hartily ffarewell, herein,

Your very loveinge ffriends,

ARTHUR CAPELL
JOHN BYRON
NICH: BYRON
AB: SHIPMAN
OR: BRIDGMAN

Chester, Dec^ber 7th 1643.

APPENDIX C

ORDER FOR A GENERAL MUSTER IN ANGLESEY

Whereas it is found necessary for the Defence of this Island that the traine Band Souldie^{rs} & others able to beare Armes should be duly exercised according to the discipline of Warre, that they may be the better enabled (by the frequent use of their Armes) for the preservatoñ of their Country, Wee doe therefore hereby desire and authorise your Lo^p: to send Orders unto your chief officers & Capt^e of the Hundrede of Tindethway, Menny, & Dunkellin, Requiring them to issue their Warrante to the high Constables of their respective Comote, comanding them to Sumon in all the able Men both horse & foote w'hin their severall Comote, to appeare on Bewmaris Greene furnished wth their best Armes, on the first day of St. John Baptist, by nyne of the Clocke in the Morning, there to be exercised as aforesayd. And in Case any should make default in their appearance, we doe hereby enable you^r Lo^p either to imprison, or impose such other punishm't upon them, as yor Lo^p shall think fitt in their behalfe. Hereof Wee expect yor Lo^p will not faile. Dated at Bewmaris.
14th Junii 1644.

> JOHN MENNES. W. BOLD.
> THO: CHEDLE. H. OWEN.
> O. WOODS. HENRIE WHYTE.
> DD: LLOYD.

To the right Ho^{ble} the Lo; Visc^t
Buckeley, Colonell of a Regim^t
of the trayned Bandes wthin the
Comte of Tindethway, Menny &
Dunkellin.

U.C.N.W. Baron Hill MSS, 5370.

APPENDIX D

RUPERT DEMANDS A LOAN

To the Right Honerable Thomas, Lord Buckley, Viscount Cassells, These—

In ye Assembly of ye Members of both Howses of Parliam^t att Oxford It was concluded by the Kinge's Majestie, and the Members there assembled that for raysing of Moneys for mainteynance of ye Armye, Letters under his Mat^{ts} signett or Prince Seale should bee directed to such Persons as are nominated by the Members of the Houses to be able to Lend and contayned in Schedules affixed to ye Commissions for Subscriptions issued unto ye respective Counties.

The Moneys to bee raised by that way of Loane in ye Six Counties of Northwales, and ye Countie of Salop the King's Majestie hath by his Letters to ye respective Sheriffs ordered to bee payd to Mee for the use of the Armye under my Command. Therefore that the present occasions of supplying the Armye requires a speedie advance of money, I doe hereby desire yo^u upon receipt hereof to pay to the Lord Arch Bishop of Yorke whome I have entreated to receive the same, the summe of *One Hundred* xx pounds, being the summe Concluded by his Majestie and ye Members of the Howses to be lent by yo^u and specified in the Schedule before mentyoned for wch yo^u shall receive a sufficient discharge upon the Prince Seale in that behalfe. In the meanetyme a discharge of soe much received by the Lord Arch Bishop of Yorke for my use and his Majesties service shall oblige me to procure such other more formal discharge as shall bee thought necessarie. Soe not doubting of yor conformitie herein.

I rest, Yo^r Lopps ffrend,

RUPERT.

Chester the first
of August 1644.

U.C.N.W. Baron Hill MSS, 5372.

APPENDIX E

COMMISSION FOR COLONEL THOMAS DAVIES

Charles R.

Right trusty and wellbeloved Wee greete you well. Wee having given our Comission to our trusty and wellbeloved Colonell Thomas Davies to raise one Regiment of ffive Hundred ffote and Dragooners for our service and the defence and security of our Counties of fflynt and Denbeigh have thought fitt to recommend unto you and to lett you know that although other persons may have received Comissions to raise forces in those parts who have therefore the precedency yet wee knowing the ability of Colonell Davies who hath served us, and our late Royall father of blessed memory in all our expeditions, cannot but esteem him fitt to have that respect as to be preferred to the Priority of Comand (especially in the County of fflynt) which our pleasure is your Lordhsipp see performed upon all occasions that may offer themselves for our service. And so we bid you heartily farewell.

ffrom our Court at Oxford this 19th of July, 1643.

To our right trusty and wellbeloved—
Arthur Lord Capell our Lieutenant Generall of
our forces in the counties of Chester, fflynt &c.

Ld. Capell.

N.L.W. Some Gwysaney Letters and Papers. p. 1.

APPENDIX F

MAURICE REQUIRES ORDNANCE

(To Lord Bukleley).

My Lord,

Upon advertizement received that his Ma^{ty} hath some peeces of Ordnance in the towne & Castle of Beau Morise I shall desire yor Lo^{pp} to give pres'nt Order that one of the best Sakars may bee sent hither for the use & safety of this City untill such tyme as it can bee provided otherwise. And for that purpose I have appointed Colonell Moystin to convoy the same from Conway to Chester. I shall onely pray yor Lo^{pp} to give speedy Order that the Sakar may be forthwth sent to Conway wch is all att present but that I am

My Lord,
Your Lo^{pps} affectionate ffreind,

MAURICE.

Chester.
28 of ffebr. 1644.

U.C.N.W. Baron Hill MSS, 5376.

APPENDIX G

PROVISIONS FOR CHESTER

ffor my Lord Buckley.

My Lord,
    I have sent unto the Comissioners of your County forr such a proportion of Provisions as are absolutely necessary forr the preservation of the Citty and Castle of Chester.

    I shall desire you therefore not to faile to take the Care and performance of this business into your hands and to see it done with all the Speede and diligence and to be assisting to the Commissiary or his Deputy who attend you to this effort.

    And I do hereby give you all power and Authority to see this my desire putt in execution and to use such means to compell all refractory and unwilling or disaffected persons to performe the same as you, in your discretion, shall think fitt and so rest
        My Lord,
                Your Lo: ffreind
                         MAURICE.

(29 Feb, 1644/5)

U.C.N.W. Baron Hill MSS, 5377.

APPENDIX H

BEAUMARIS AND HOLYHEAD NEGLECTED

Whereas I am informed that the Castle of Beaumaris and fort raised att Holyhead are very much neglected being not garnished with men provisions and armes nor such guardes kept and duty performed which is necessary for the securing of the same and that the Cannon in eyther or both of them lieth unmounted and uselesse

These are strictly to require Tho: Lord Bulkeley in whose hands I am informed the Castle of Beaumaris now is and Owen Woods Esq., into whose care I am also informed the fort att Holyhead is committeed, to see that both the sayd Castles and forts be garnished with soldiers and provisions and the cannon mounted and all necessaries supplied according to the care required in so high a concernement.

And of this I desire the sayd Lord Bulkeley and Owen Woods Esq. not to fayle as they will answere the contrary upon theyr lives.

Given under my hand this 25° of ffebr.

1644.

MAURICE.

To the Lord Bulkeley & Owen
Woods Esq. att Beaumaris or
elsewhere.

APPENDIX I

Sir Thomas Salusbury was with his regiment at the capture of Brentford as the following extract from the *Memoirs of the Civil War* by John Gwyn of Trelydan testifies.

'The very first day that five comrades of us repaired from the Court of Richmond to the King's Royal Army, which we met accidentally that morning upon Hounslow Heath, we had no sooner put ourselves into rank and file under the command of our worthy old acquaintance Sir George Bunckley, then major to Sir Thomas Salsbury, but we marched up to the enemy, engaged them by Sir Richard Winn's house and the Thames side, beat them to retreat into Brainford, beat them from the one Brainford to the other, and from thence to the open field.'

(Copied from Montgomery Collections. xiv. p. 329.)

BIBLIOGRAPHY

MANUSCRIPT SOURCES

Rhual MSS and Documents (1949). National Library of Wales.
Gwysaney Manuscripts. University College of North Wales.
Baron Hill Manuscripts. University College of North Wales.
Kinmel Manuscripts and Documents. University College of North
    Wales.
Quarter Sessions Records. Caernarvonshire County Archives.
Presentments. Caernarvonshire County Archives.
Unpublished thesis. *Sea Power and Welsh History*. Aled Eames M.A.
Pedigree of the Morgans of Golden Grove, prepared by the late H. R.
    Hughes Esquire of Kinmel Hall.
The history of the family of Heaton of Plas Heaton. (Family MS.).
Gwysaney Deeds, Documents and Papers. National Library of Wales.
The Family Papers of Owen and Stanley of Penrhos, Holyhead.
    University College of North Wales.

PRINTED SOURCES

Calendar of State Papers, Domestic.
Calendar of the Committee for Compounding.
Calendar of Salusbury Correspondence (edited by W. H. Smith M.A.),
    Board of Celtic Studies, History & Law Series No. xiv.
Calendar of Wynn (of Gwydir) Papers, 1515-1690. (edited by Sir
    John Ballinger), National Library of Wales.
List of Sheriffs of Wales. Public Record Office.
Dictionary of National Biography.
Pedigrees of the Anglesey and Caernarvonshire Families. J. E. Griffith.
    (1914).
Cromwell's Army. Sir Charles Firth.
Chester and North Wales Archaeological and Historic Society *Journal*
    Vol. XXV. *The Siege of Chester* by the late Canon Rupert Morris,
    M.A., D.D., edited and completed by P. H. Lawson, A.R.I.B.A.
    (1923).
An Account of the castle and town of Ruthin. R. Newcome. (1829).
An Account of the castle and town of Denbigh. R. Newcome (1829).
Memoirs of the Civil War in Wales and the Marches. J. Roland
    Phillips. (1874).
Ancient and Modern Denbigh. J. Williams. (1856).
Historic Notices of the Borough and County-town of Flint. Henry
    Taylor. (1883).
History of the City of Chester. Joseph Hemingway. (1831).
Studies in Stuart Wales. A. H. Dodd, M.A., F.R. Hist. S.
Mitre and Musket. B. Dew Roberts. (1938).
Royal Visits and Progresses to Wales. E. Parry. (1850).

The Ottley Papers. Shropshire Archaeological Society.

A History of Wem. S. Garbett. (1740).

A History of Shrewsbury. H. Owen and J. B. Blakeley. (1825).

Diary of the Marches of the Royal Army during the Great Civil War. Richard Symonds. (1839). Camden Series. Royal Historical Soc.

The Parliamentary History of Wales. W. R. Williams. (1895).

A History of the Puritan Movement in Wales. Thomas Richards, M.A., D.Lit. (1920).

Memorials of English Affairs. Bulstrode Whitelock. (1853).

Religious Development in Wales. (1923). Thomas Richards.

History of Hawarden (1822). Richard Willett.

Montgomeryshire Worthies.

History of the 13 townships of the old parish of Wrexham. (1903). A. N. Palmer.

History of the Parish Church of Wrexham. A. N. Palmer.

Old Wales.

History of the Great Civil War. S. R. Gardiner.

Oliver Cromwell. John Buchan.

A History of Nantwich. J. Hall. (1883).

Progress of the Duke of Beaufort through North Wales in 1684. T. Dineley. (1883).

A Record of Caernarvonshire, 1809-11. E. Hyde Hall. Caernarvonshire Historical Society. Record Series No. 2.

The Heart of Northern Wales. W. Bezant Lowe, M.A.

Scrinia Reserata (Life of Archbishop John Williams), John Hacket. (1693).

Conway Castle and Town Walls, A. J. Taylor, M.A., F.S.A., F.R. Hist. S. (Ministry of Works).

Tours in Wales. Thomas Pennant. (1883).

The History of Chirk and Chirkland. Margaret Mahler. (1912).

Honourable Society of Cymmrodorion. *Transactions.*

1927-28. John Williams of Gloddaeth. Judge Ivor Bowen.

1930-31. The Second Civil War in Wales. Sir Frederick Rees.

Archaeologia Cambrensis.

1846. Diary of William Maurice.

1869. Unpublished Correspondence between Archbishop Williams and the Marquis of Ormonde.

1887. Correspondence during the Great Rebellion. (Welsh compounders).

A Tourist's Guide through the County of Caernarvon. P. B. Williams. (1821). Appendix gives Charles 1's letters to Commissioners of Array.

Anglesey Antiquarian Society and Field Club. Transactions.

1948. Colonel Richard Bulkeley's death. (from N.L.W. MSS 9080E).

1952. Anglesey in the Civil War. A. H. Dodd.

Denbighshire Historical Society Transactions.

1954. The Civil War in East Denbighshire. A. H. Dodd.

1955. John Robinson, Civil War Colonel. Norman Tucker.
1956. Denbigh's Loyal Governor. Norman Tucker.
Flintshire Historical Society's Publications.
1916-17. Articles for the surrender of Flint Castle. H. Taylor.
1952-53. Flintshire and the Puritan movement. T. Richards.
1953-54. Flintshire Politics and the 17th Century. A. H. Dodd.
1957 Colonel Sir Roger Mostyn, First Baronet, Norman Tucker.
Caernarvonshire Historical Society's Transactions.
1948. Culverins for Charles. Norman Tucker.
1949. Some Pages from the History of Pant Glas, Ysbyty Ifan. R. T. Jenkins, O.B.E., M.A., D.Litt.
1952. Civil War Colonel, Sir John Carter. Norman Tucker.
1953. Caernarvonshire and the Civil War. A. H. Dodd.
1955. Sea Power and Caernarvonshire. Aled Eames M.A.
Llandudno, Colwyn Bay and District Field Club Proceedings.
1953. Captain Morgan's Lonely Grave. Norman Tucker.
The Parish Registers of Conway. Alice Hadley. (1900).
A short Relation of a Long Journey. (1652). John Taylor.
The Dissenters Burial Ground, Wrexham. G. Vernon Price, M.B.E., F.R.G.S.

ACKNOWLEDGEMENT

THE writer wishes gratefully to acknowledge his indebtedness to the following:

The Rt. Hon. LORD BAGOT for permission to photograph the portrait of Colonel William Salesbury at Blithfield.

Mr. A. D. H. PENNANT, Nantlys, for the inclusion of the miniatures of Wm. Robinson and Colonel John Robinson, the portrait of Major David Pennant, and the plan of Holt bridge,

Mr. W. W. HARRIS and Mr. E. EMRYS JONES for their photographs,

The BRITISH MUSEUM for the print of Sir John Owen,

Miss MOFFAT and Miss HILL, Gloddaeth Hall, for permission to photograph the portrait of Col. Hugh Wynne,

Mr. CLARENCE ELLIS, M.A., F.R.HIST.S, for scrutinizing the page-proofs,

Mr. FRANK PRICE JONES, B.A., honorary editor of the Denbighshire Historical Society, and Miss K. M. COOKS, F.L.A., honorary secretary of the Llandudno, Colwyn Bay and District Field Club, for the loan of blocks,

Dr. S. W. PATTERSON (Ruthin Castle Limited) for use of the copyright photograph of Ruthin Castle,

The NATIONAL MUSEUM OF WALES for allowing the reproduction of the portrait of Colonel Thomas Madryn,

Mr. CHARLES W. HOWARTH, R.C.A., for the battlefield maps, and line drawings,

Mr. ASA DAVIES, for assisting with the indexing, and Messrs. GEE & SON, LTD., for their efficient co-operation.

INDEX — PERSONS

DALLISON, Sir Thos., 51
Danske, Capt., 110
Davenport, Ralph (Lancs.), 142
Davenport, Thos. (Flints.), 151
Davies, Lt.-Col. Thos, 10, 18, 21, 43-4, 64, 169, 179 (commission)
Davies, Robt. (Gwysaney), 164, 170
Denbigh, EARL of, 50-1
Derby, EARL of, 152, 160
Derbyshire Horse, 85-6
Digby, LORD, 64-5, 79, 81, 92
Disney, Lt.-Col., 100
Dodd, Prof. A. H., 15, 62, 140, 155, 157
Dolben, Major John, 53, 147-9, 151, 160, 169
Dolben, Robt. 34
Duckenfield, Col. R., 139
Dutton, Capt. Rd., 160, 169.

EAMES, Aled, 112
Eaton, Capt., 33
Edwardes, John, 37-9, 126
Edwardes, Thos., 99, 123, 126
Edwards, "Baron" Evan, 66-9, 85
Edwards, Isaac, 143
Edwards, Capt. John, 160, 169
Edwards, Harry, 132
Edwards, Richd. (Commissary), 50
Edwards, Capt. Wm. (Alderman), 66, 68, 85
Edwards, Capt. Wm. (Chirkland), 126, 132
Ellice, Col. Robt., 10, 21, 31-3, 39
Ellis, Capt. Andrew, 16
Elliot, Major, 104
English-Irish Army, 43, 47, 59, 110
Ernley, Sir Michael, 43, 52-3
Essex, EARL of, 20, 27
Evans, Rev. Michael, 150
Evans, Trumpeter, 161
Evans, Robert, 28
Evet, Major, 91
Eyton, John (sen.), Leeswood, 169 (junr.) 124, 169
Eyton, Kenrick, 37, 124
Eyton, Sir Robt., 99
Eyton, Sir Thos., 103
Eyton, Capt. Wm., 151.

FAIRFAX, Sir Thomas (LORD), 20, 49, 69, 129-30, 149
Fairfax, Sir Wm., 53
Farrar, Capt. Robt., 123
Finch, Capt., 85

Firth, Sir Chas., 18-21
Floyd (see Lloyd)
Foulkes, Mr. Robt., 128, Serg. Richd., 50
Fortiscue, Sir Faithful, 151
Fowler, Mr. Richd., 63
Fox, Capt. Gilbert, 142.

GAMULL, Sir Francis, 75-6
Gardiner, Sir Thos., 52
Gerard LORD (Sir Chas.), 74, 76
Gerard Sir Wm., 170
Gerrard, Lt.-Col. G., 68-9
Gerrard, Col., 156
Gethin, Capt., 104
Gibson, Maj.-Gen. Rd., 43
Gilmor, Maj., 33
Glynne, Serjeant, John, 99
Glynne, Col. Thos., 21 99-100
Glynne, Thos. (Plasnewydd), 166
Goodman, Edw., 169
Goring, General, 155
Gottenby, Capt. N. (Prosperous) 112
Green Howards, 20
Griffith, John, 25
Griffith, Piers, 97
Griffith, Mr. Thos., 151; Thos. (Llanaelhaiarn), 132
Griffith, Wm. (surgeon), 137-8
Griffith, Wm. (Dr.), Carreglwyd, 110, 150
Griffiths, Maurice (servant to Sir J. Owen), 142
Griffiths, Lieut. 53
Griffiths, Lieut-Col. Peter, 89, 92, 123, 169
Guilson, Capt. J. (Leopard Merchant), 112
Gustavus Adolphus, 10
Gwynn, Sir Rd. (see Wynne).

HACKET, Bishop J., 45, 103, 108, 155
Hadley, Miss Alice, 168
Hall, E. Hyde, 107, 137
Hamilton, DUKE of, 146, 149-50, 155
Hamond, Major Ed. 43
Hampden, John 20
Hancock, Capt., 154
Hanmer, Sir, John, 164
Hanmer, Sir Thomas, 18, 32-3
Hanmer, Thomas (Apley Castle), 170
Hanmer, Roger, 123
Hanmer, Wm. (Fenhall), 164, 170

Hanmer, Widow, 66
Harlech, LORD, 155
Harrison, John, 142
Harrison, Rev. Wm. 19n
Harward, Humphrey, 143n
Henry, Rev. Philip, 15
Herbert, LORD (Cherbury), 52
Herbert, Morgan, 134, Capt. Edw. 134
Herbert, Richard, Esq., 164
Hokesworth, Major, 85
Holt, Capt., 85
Holland, EARL, 155
Holland, Elizabeth 155
Hookes, Lt.-Col. Hugh, 151, Lieut. Hugh, 151n
Hookes, Lieut. Nicholas, 50
Hookes, Alderman William, 33
Hotham, Sir John, 24
Hughes, Lt.-Col. 134
Hughes, Capt. Robt. 151

JAMES 1 KING, 72
Jefferise (Jeffries) Evan, 158
Johnes, Capt., 33, 40
Jones, Col., 106, 139
Jones, Humffrey, J.P., 131
Jones, Rev. Hugo, 168
Jones, John (sen.) Halkyn, 169
Jones, Col. John (Maesygarnedd), 16, 29, 99, 106, 147, 151
Jones, Col. Michael, 63, 65-6, 70, 75, 83
Jones, Q'master, Owen, 50
Jones, Wm. (Gent.), 166

KING (see Charles)
Kyffin, Watkin, 32
Kynaston, Capt. James, 134, 142
Kynaston, Lieutn. Thos., 157-9, 167-8

LAMBERT, Gen. J., 157, 160-1
Langdale, Sir M., 74-78
Laugharne, Maj.-Gen. R., 149
Lee, Col., 134
Lewes, Michael, 110, 176
Lewis, Thos., David Thos., Wm. Thos., 131
Lichfield, EARL of, 73, 76
Lloyd, Capt. (Swan, frigate), 112, 115
Lloyd, Cornet, 50
Lloyd, Capt. Penhwnllys, 153
Lloyd, Bevis Esq., 164
Lloyd, David (soldier), 173
Lloyd, Maj. David, 99-100, 177

Lloyd, Sir Edw. 164
Lloyd, Edw. (Mold) & Thos. (his son), 169
Lloyd, John, Esq. (Denbs.), 164; John Esq. (Merioneth), 164
Lloyd, Capt. Luke, 16, 133
Lloyd, Mr. Matthias, 142
Lloyd, Pierce Esq., 164
Lloyd, Col. Richard, Llwyn-y-Maen, 134, 142-4, 170
Lloyd, Col. Sir Richd. Esclus, 13, 18, 24 (knighted 27), 29, 37, 75, 125-8.
Lloyd, Roger Esq., 164
Lloyd, Lieut. Thos., 142
Lloyd, Sheriff William, Plashen, 22, 99, 134-140n, 143-4
Lloyd, Mr. (J.P.), 166
Llwyd, Morgan, 15
Louthian, Col. Jas., 68, 75, 153-4
Lucas, Sir Chas., 80, 91
Lupton, 18.

MADRIN, Capt., 139
Madryn, Capt. John, 50
Madryn, Col. Thos., 21, 33, 99, 131, 135, 159, 161-2
Malbon, Thos., 40, 47, 93, 128n, 170
Manley, Maj. Francis, 22, 37, 51, 124, 163, 170
Manley, Maj. John, 22, 163
Marrow, Col. John, 50-2
Mason, Col. Thos., 16, 123, 166
Mathews, Mr. John, 142
Maurice PRINCE, 60-3, 80, 86, 180-2
Maurice, Wm., diarist, 32, 60, 87, 93, 98, 122, 147, 149
Meldrum, Sir John, 51-3
Mennes, Sir John, 177
Monck, Col. Geo., 49
Montrose, MARQUIS of, 73, 77, 81
Moore, Maj. Edw., 126
Morgan, Capt. Edw., Golden Grove, 94, 161
Morgan, Capt., 53, 134, 139
Morgan, Lieut., 53
Morgan, Ensign, 50
Morgan, Capt. John, 151
Morgan, Rev. Robt., 150
Morris, Capt. Hugh, 94
Morris, Lewis, 166-7
Morrys, Capt., 33
Mostyn, Sir Edw., 164
Mostyn, John, 101
Mostyn, Sir Roger, knt., 24

INDEX — PLACES

194

195

QUEEN'S College, Oxford, 45

RAGLAN, 73
Red CASTLE (see Powys)
Red Hill Park, 152-3
Rhewl, 94
Rhual, 66, 69, 85
Rhuddlan CASTLE, 11, 42, 82, 89, 92, 101-2, 120, 125, 128, 133, 165; town, 11, 42
Ryland March, 11
Rhydolion, 15
Rowton Moor, 17, 81, 100; battle of 74-80
Rug, 122, 169, Rhug, 173
Ruabon, 55n
Ruthin CASTLE, 9, 11, 34, 41, 47, 51-2, 55-6, 60-3, 79-80, 83-5, 92; Surrendered 94-5; 117, 124-5, 128, 133, 151.

SCOTS, 13, 23, 46
Scottish campaign, 24
Scottish coast, 115
Segrwyd, 147, 160, 169
Severn river, 32
Shrewsbury, 9, 12, 25-7, 29, 31-2, 34, 36, 49, 51-2, 60, 63 (captured)
Snowdon, 73, 134
St. Asaph, 65, 70, 147
St. Beuno's, 156
St. Chad's, 36
St. George's Channel, 109
St. Hilary's, 79
St. Mary's (Beaumaris), 152
St. Marcella (Whitchurch), 83.

TALYBOLION, 154
Tarvin, 52

Tindaethwy, 177
Towyn, 134
Traeth Coch, 154
Trefnant, 82
Trefriw, 129
Tregarnedd, 101
Tros-yn-Afon, 153
Turnham Green, 28
Twthill (Caern.), 97.

VAENOL (Vaynol), 22, 29, 99, 131

WARRINGTON, 35, 160
Warwick Horse, 85-6
Welshpool, 51, 129
Wem, 32, 35-7, 48, 55, 170
Westminster, 46, 160, 164
Whitchurch (Denbigh), 83-5, 89, 95, 123, 172
Whitchurch (Salop), 35, 50
Whitford, 151
Wigfair (Wickwer), 70
Windsor CASTLE, 149
Winnington Bridge, 161
Wirral (Worrall), 41
Woodhey, 37
Woodlands, The, 106
Worcester, 46, 61, 91
Wortenburgh, 170
Wrexham, 9, 11, 15, 24-7, 29-31, 35, 39-41, 48, 60-1, 63, 69, 89, 93, 99, 133, 160-2.

YNYSKYNHAYNON, 172
York, 21, 24, 72
Yorkshiremen, 42, 53, 66
Yorkshire Horse, 69
Yr Wylfa, 110
Ystrad, 122.